Your Guide to 40 Days of Prayer & Fasting

Your Guide to 40 Days of Prayer & Fasting

Daniel W. Evans

Tate Publishing & *Enterprises*

I dedicate this book in memory of my dad, Martin W. Evans, who went home to be with the Lord on the 18th day of May 2003. He was a faithful and powerful man of God. Using his faith in Christ Jesus was a way of life for him. There was never a person he met who was a stranger. He would be able to get them to open up to him in a way that would allow him to testify of his many answered prayers and then witness to them of Christ's redemptive power. His prayer life was consistent, powerful, and impressive. I have seen many prayers answered for him and for many others whom he had prayed for. He was a tremendous example to many others and me. He is truly missed and has left behind a legacy that will glorify God and will continue to produce works that will follow him. My dad and mom, Ola H. Evans, were great examples for my sister, Joan, brothers, Samuel and Michael, and myself. Even though we may be separated by the distance between heaven and earth, we will all be together again one day.

We will be praying for you!

Foreword

At first I wasn't sure if I would be the right person to write the foreword for this guide. After I prayed about it, I knew I would do it justice because there is no wrong way to testify of God and His awesomeness and how my life has been impacted.

I have known Daniel (Danny) for twelve years, and in that time he has played an important role in helping me completely turn my life around. He is different from many people you will ever meet or be associated with. His beliefs are true to God's Word, and because of that example, it was easier for me to yield to God's will for my life and live every day for him. Danny's love for God is as deep as deep can go!

Have you ever met someone and wondered if they were really the person they appeared to be? You know, you wonder if they are different when they are around others and family? I know I have, but some things just cannot be played off or faked. Danny's dedication to God and his love for others are reflected through his actions, not just sometimes, but all the time! He has a way of helping you understand God's Word when it is probably the last thing you want to understand, much less listen to, or talk about. With passion and determination to share the Word of

God without judging, he takes his knowledge from the Bible with his experiences and shows you it is from God, not his own opinion or thought.

My walk with God is stronger and gets stronger every day. I strive to continue to learn more, and listening to Danny's teachings and sermons have helped me tremendously, rather they be in person at churches and revivals or on cassette tapes or CDs. Sharing his knowledge has shown me how to read and study my Bible. His endeavors have opened my eyes to many things I never understood or even thought that I wanted to understand. I'm sure I am not alone when speaking on this subject, but I don't know anyone who likes taking part in something that reveals their failures, mistakes, or anything that challenges them to make something right.

That is why I knew I had to take the challenge and practice prayer and fasting by using, *Your Guide to 40 Days of Prayer & Fasting.*

I knew how to pray, but I never really knew, or I guess you could say understood, the discipline of fasting. Danny took time to show me Scripture and references in the Bible regarding prayer and fasting and explained why practicing it is so important. The good part is, he included helpful information in the guide, which is great, because I always have questions, and he is not always there to answer them.

I trust Danny because I know him, and I know his love for God. He has witnessed and been part of many blessings and miracles and has led many in prayer who have invited Jesus into their hearts. Not everyone will sacrifice their time to serve God and share His Word in everything they do. Danny's work comes from his heart, and his love for God is reflected in his fruits.

Trust me, as with any product by Daniel Evans, you will be blessed. Don't be surprised if your views about life, your attitude, and your surroundings start changing. I promise it will be a great experience!

—Angel J. Register

Introduction & Instructions

Since 1982, I have been practicing fasting on a regular basis from a meal at a time, to hours, days, and even weeks, and have always found this discipline to be very rewarding. The partial to complete abstinence of food has always been a part of my fasting periods, along with other activities and pleasures of the flesh. The act of self-denial has been very beneficial to my mind, body, and relationship with God. While exercising this spiritual discipline, I am more aware of my relationship with God because I am denying the desires of the flesh, which at times may hinder my deep focus on him. Because of this, fasting helps the soul (mind, will, and emotions) to stay focused on God instead of on the world and the body's fleshly desires. I have gained self-control over many areas of my life through fasting and have never allowed it to become a habit, so that it may always be a conscious decision to fast and seek God. This voluntary practice allows me to build and maintain my relationship with him.

My studies of the Word of God have revealed to me that the spiritual discipline of fasting itself is more important than naming specific biblical examples of fasting and using them only for certain needs. For example, using a twenty-one-day fast and naming it a "Daniel Fast" may not necessarily bring you understanding of a vision (Daniel 10), but will assist you in developing the Daniel kind of character that will prepare you to receive from God as Daniel and many other biblical characters did as they fasted. As you read further, I will show you examples of people in the Word of God who fasted and received from God. These examples do not set a standard procedural format but are to be used as examples only to enlighten the reader of the benefits of self-denial of the flesh to seek and please God.

I have also taught on this subject and referenced it in my preaching on many occasions. The idea of this guide came when I was asked to prepare a structured fasting program for my home church, Living Waters Christian Community, Durham, North Carolina. When I started the writing, it flowed from the Holy Spirit until I completed the program. During the fasting period, the Lord spoke to me and told me to have the guide published for others who are seeking structure to start or to continue fasting. In this guide, you will find scripture with explanations, introductions, and daily help that will equip you to understand fasting and how to develop your own servitude to God by fasting. From personal experiences of recording what had been revealed to me during my own fasting times was also incorporated into this book for your benefit as well. Remember, fasting helps you to develop a deeper, intimate, and more personal relationship between the Father, the Son, and yourself. Now, let us get started with your divine appointment!

This is a personal guide to help you through your forty days of prayer and fasting. As a personal guide, you can record what is revealed to you, for you; many times people forget to write down the revelations or directions they receive from the Lord. In this 40-day guide, spaces have been provided to assist you as you write each day. It is recorded in the Bible that the prophets were often commanded by the Lord to write what they had seen or heard. The purpose was not for them only, but for future readers as well. It is especially good to write down what you receive from the Lord, because if you are like me, you can't always rely on your memory. Also, you can be sure that if God has given you something that will change your life, the devil will work overtime by bringing things into your life to help you to forget or persuade you to cover it up with the cares of this world.

This 40-day guide includes scripture from the King James, New International, New American Standard, Amplified, and New King James versions of the Bible. As you read and pray each passage, the Holy Spirit may lead you to go to the Word of God and read the passages before and after the listed Scripture. This is when you may receive rebuke, correction, instruction, revelation, or direction. In 2 Timothy 3:16–17 (AMP) it says, "Every Scripture is God-breathed (given by his inspiration) and profitable for instruction, for reproof *and* conviction of sin, for correction of error *and* discipline in obedience, [and] for training in righteousness (in holy living, in conformity to God's will in thought, purpose, and action), So that the man of God may be complete *and* proficient, well fitted *and* thoroughly equipped for every good work." Also, 2 Peter 1:20–21 (AMP) says, "[Yet] first [you must] understand this, that no prophecy of Scripture is [a matter] of any personal *or* private *or* special interpretation (loosening, solving). For no prophecy ever originated because some man willed it [to do so—it never came by human impulse], but men spoke from God who were borne along (moved and impelled) by the Holy Spirit."

As you pray and allow the Holy Spirit to assist you in what you should fast and sacrifice, you can log each item in this guide. You will find spaces to record your commitments for each activity, entertainment, pleasure, and food that you will be fasting and sacrificing during the forty days of prayer and fasting. You can also record the times for the activities or meals, as applicable. What you fast, how often you fast, and how many different things you fast are between you and the Holy Spirit. According to the Scripture, we do find that food is always involved in fasting. So, whether you sacrifice activities or not, food should be included in your fasting. The decision whether you fast a meal, certain types of food, or all food for the entire fasting period is still between you and the Holy Spirit. Whatever is decided, your commitment is what will make a successful fast for you. Read the Scripture and comments below for some examples of biblical characters fasting for different reasons.

- PSALM 35:13 (KJV) *"But as for me, when they were sick, my clothing was sackcloth: I humbled my soul with fasting; and my prayer returned into mine own bosom."*

Fasting can enhance your prayers for the sick and will humble your soul, which is your mind, will, and emotions.

- PSALM 69:10 (KJV) *"When I wept, and chastened my soul with fasting, that was to my reproach."*

Some use fasting to discipline themselves and for correction when found in sin.

- JEREMIAH 36:6 (KJV) *"Therefore go thou, and read in the roll, which thou hast written from my mouth, the words of the LORD in the ears of the people in the LORD's house upon the fasting day: and also thou shalt read them in the ears of all Judah that come out of their cities."*

Reading Scripture is common during fasting, and with prayer included it will bring better understanding and revelation. It is good to read Scripture aloud during your fasting, because it may help you have an even better understanding when hearing it.

- DANIEL 6:18 (KJV) *"Then the king went to his palace, and passed the night fasting: neither were instruments of music brought before him: and his sleep went from him."*

When you fast, you may choose to not sleep but instead spend time in prayer as Jesus did on several occasions. Here in this scripture music is a pleasure that the king sacrificed during his fasting.

- DANIEL 9:3 (KJV) *"And I set my face unto the Lord God, to seek by prayer and supplications, with fasting, and sackcloth, and ashes..."*

Seeking God is one of the greatest things you can do during your prayer and fasting and should be a common practice in your prayer closet times. Seeking God's face rather than his provision will produce a deep, intimate relationship with him.

- DANIEL 10:2–3 (KJV) *"In those days I Daniel was mourning three full weeks. I ate no pleasant bread, neither came flesh nor wine in my mouth, neither did I anoint myself at all, till three whole weeks were fulfilled."*

Sacrificing food during prayer and fasting is a practice often mentioned in Scripture, as Daniel did in these passages. Daniel also fasted three whole weeks awaiting his answer from the Lord. If you study Daniel 10, you will find that his answer was sent on the day he started praying, but battles in the heavenlies (spirit realm) between the angelic messenger and demons prevented Daniel's answer from being delivered until three whole weeks later. Daniel remained faithful and committed to his fasting and was constantly seeking God until he received his answer.

- MATTHEW 6:16–18 (KJV) *"Moreover when ye fast, be not, as the hypocrites, of a sad countenance: for they disfigure their faces, that they may appear unto men to fast. Verily I say unto you, they have their reward. But thou, when thou fastest, anoint thine head, and wash thy face; That thou appear not unto men to fast, but unto thy Father which is in secret: and thy Father, which seeth in secret, shall reward thee openly."*

When you fast with the proper motives, you can expect rewards and answered prayer. Fasting should bring joy and be accomplished with joy; only a result that your faith in God can bring forth.

- MARK 9:29 (KJV) *"And he said unto them, this kind can come forth by nothing, but by prayer and fasting."*

Some things will not be received or accomplished without prayer and fasting. If you study more of Mark 9, you will find that casting out devils is the subject referenced in this passage.

- LUKE 2:37 (KJV) *"And she was a widow of about fourscore and four years, which departed not from the temple, but served God with fastings and prayers night and day."*

There are some who serve God through fasting and prayers regularly. They fast and pray for many different people for many different reasons. The door of opportunity is always opened by the Holy Spirit for them to fast and pray and to come in agreement with others on their behalf. Some of these servants of God spend a lot of time developing a deep, intimate, and awesome relationship with their heavenly Father and the Lord Jesus Christ.

- ACTS 10:30 (KJV) *"And Cornelius said, 'Four days ago I was fasting until this hour; and at the ninth hour I prayed in my house, and, behold, a man stood before me in bright clothing...'"*

Prayer and fasting will not only bring revelations

of the Word of God to you, but specific directions and an understanding of God's will. So many seek his will and purpose for their lives but with the wrong motives and while in sin. This causes them to become disappointed, discouraged, and confused. If you pray and fast to develop a deeper and more personal relationship with him, you will find his will and purpose for your life.

- ACTS 13:2 (KJV) *"As they ministered to the Lord, and fasted, the Holy Ghost said, 'Separate me Barnabas and Saul for the work whereunto I have called them.'"*

You will be attentive to the voice of the Lord when you serve him while fasting. His calling and direction for you will be made known, and you will receive divine connections to fulfill the calling on your life.

- 1 CORINTHIANS 7:5 (KJV) *"Defraud ye not one the other, except it be with consent for a time, that ye may give yourselves to fasting and prayer; and come together again, that Satan tempt you not for your incontinency."*

Let's look at the Amplified Bible translation of this verse. *"Do not refuse and deprive and defraud each other [of your due marital rights], except perhaps by mutual consent for a time, so that you may devote yourselves unhindered to prayer. But afterwards resume marital relations, lest Satan tempt you [to sin] through your lack of restraint of sexual desire."* In other words, some will fast the sexual relations of their marriage, but only with consent of the spouse.

In the back of this guide, you will find a place to write prayer requests. Before you start your prayer and fasting, write the requests from others for whom you have been praying. As you go through your prayer and fasting period, the Holy Spirit will speak to others to give you their prayer requests, because your praying will be more intense and you will be a stronger warrior in the spirit realm. As you log each request, before and during your fasting period, intercede for these requests daily. There are also spaces provided to write praise reports for answered prayers.

If you are part of a church or group participating in this prayer and fasting endeavor, it is important to pray for one another on a daily basis. Most assuredly, Satan will attack when you are willing to sacrifice things the flesh desires. He knows that these sacrifices are evidence of a sincere heart, and that you are serious about developing a deeper relationship with God. Praying for one another will strengthen the entire group and encourage them to keep their commitments and move deeper in God. A separate page is provided in the back of this guide for you to list the names of those who have also committed to this fasting endeavor with you, along with any other information that you may desire to write about that particular person.

When using this 40-day prayer and fasting guide, you will find three boxes at the top of each page for you to check whether you *Prayed, Fasted, Read and Prayed Scripture,* or all three. Also, for each day, boxes are provided for you to check beside each passage of Scripture as you read and pray each one. This guide is not intended to create a perfect fasting process, a successful fast, or to make a spiritual giant out of you. It is a guide to assist you in your commitments and to keep a record of everything that transpired during your fast. This is your personal guide, which can be kept for future reference.

The verse below is my prayer for you as you go through your forty days of prayer and fasting. May you prosper in your body, mind, and spirit by glorifying God in all that you do!

> *"Beloved, I pray that you may prosper in every way and [that your body] may keep well, even as [I know] your soul keeps well and prospers."*
>
> 3 John 1:2 (AMP)

By His Divine Touch,

Daniel Evans

Daniel Evans
President / Divine Touch, Inc.

Start date of your prayer and fasting

_____ / _____ / _____

_____

Write Your Name Here

Your Personal Writings!

List below the activities, entertainment, food(s), meals, etc., with times, as applicable, that you will fast and/or sacrifice during the forty days of prayer and fasting.

Fasting / Sacrificing Items   *Day, Time, etc.*

1. _____   1. _____

2. _____   2. _____

3. _____   3. _____

4. _____   4. _____

5. _____   5. _____

6. _____   6. _____

7. _____   7. _____

List below the things you are seeking from God during your prayer and fasting.

1. _____

2. _____

3. _____

4. _____

5. _____

6. _____

7. _____

8. _____

9. _____

10. _____

Use the spaces below for additional information you need to record.

1. _____   1. _____

2. _____   2. _____

3. _____   3. _____

4. _____   4. _____

5. _____   5. _____

6. _____   6. _____

7. _____   7. _____

8. _____   8. _____

9. _____   9. _____

10. _____   10. _____

11. _____   11. _____

12. _____   12. _____

Before you start your prayer and fasting period, let us review three examples of forty days and forty nights of fasting from the Word of God.

• • •

1) Moses spent time with the Lord and fasted for forty days and forty nights to receive commandments from the Lord.

Moses went back a second time, spent time with the Lord, and fasted forty days and forty nights to receive the same commandments again.

> "And *he was there with the* LORD *forty days and forty nights; he did neither eat bread, nor drink water.* And he wrote upon the tables the words of the covenant, the Ten Commandments."
>
> Exodus 34:28 (NIV)

"At the end of the forty days and forty nights, the LORD gave me the two stone tablets, the tablets of the covenant. Then the LORD told me, "Go down from here at once, because your people whom you brought out of Egypt have become corrupt. They have turned away quickly from what I commanded them and have made a cast idol for themselves." And the LORD said to me, "I have seen this people, and they are a stiff-necked people indeed! Let me alone, so that I may destroy them and blot out their name from under heaven. And I will make you into a nation stronger and more numerous than they." So I turned and went down from the mountain while it was ablaze with fire. And the two tablets of the covenant were in my hands. When I looked, I saw that you had sinned against the LORD your God; you had made for yourselves an idol cast in the shape of a calf. You had turned aside quickly from the way that the LORD had commanded you. So I took the two tablets and threw them out of my hands, breaking them to pieces before your eyes. *Then once again I fell prostrate before the LORD for forty days and forty nights; I ate no bread and drank no water,* because of all the sin you had committed, doing what was evil in the LORD's sight and so provoking him to anger. I feared the anger and wrath of the LORD, for he was angry enough with you to destroy you. But again the LORD listened to me."

Deuteronomy 9:11–19 (NIV)

2) While Elijah rested in despair, an angel visited him twice and provided him with food. The rest and food he received gave him strength to fast during his entire forty-day and forty-night journey.

> While he himself went a day's journey into the desert. He came to a broom tree, sat down under it and prayed that he might die. "I have had enough, LORD," he said. "Take my life; I am no better than my ancestors." Then he lay down under the tree and fell asleep. All at once an angel touched him and said, "Get up and eat." he looked around, and there by his head was a cake of bread baked over hot coals, and a jar of water. He ate and drank and then lay down again. The angel of the LORD came back a second time and touched him and said, "Get up and eat, for the journey is too much for you." *So he got up and ate and drank. Strengthened by that food, he traveled forty days and forty nights* until he reached Horeb, the mountain of God. There he went into a cave and spent the night. And the word of the LORD came to him: "What are you doing here, Elijah?" he replied, "I have been very zealous for the LORD God Almighty. The Israelites have rejected your covenant, broken down your altars, and put your prophets to death with the sword. I am the only one left, and now they are trying to kill me too." The LORD said, "Go out and stand on the mountain in the presence of the LORD,

for the LORD is about to pass by." Then a great and powerful wind tore the mountains apart and shattered the rocks before the LORD, but the LORD was not in the wind. After the wind there was an earthquake, but the LORD was not in the earthquake. After the earthquake came a fire, but the LORD was not in the fire. And after the fire came a gentle whisper. When Elijah heard it, he pulled his cloak over his face and went out and stood at the mouth of the cave. Then a voice said to him, "What are you doing here, Elijah?" he replied, "I have been very zealous for the LORD God Almighty. The Israelites have rejected your covenant, broken down your altars, and put your prophets to death with the sword. I am the only one left, and now they are trying to kill me too.

1 Kings 19:4–14 (NIV)

• • •

3) Jesus was led by the Spirit into the wilderness to fast, be tempted of the devil, and prove the Word of God for forty days and forty nights.

"Then Jesus was led by the Spirit into the desert to be tempted by the devil. *After fasting forty days and forty nights, he was hungry.* The tempter came to him and said, "If you are the Son of God, tell these stones to become bread." Jesus answered, "It is written: 'Man does not live on bread alone, but on every word that comes from the mouth of God." Then the devil took him to the holy city and had him stand on the highest point of the temple. "If you are the Son of God," he said, "throw yourself down. For it is written: 'he will command his angels concerning you, and they will lift you up in their hands, so that you will not strike your foot against a stone.'" Jesus answered him, "It is also written: 'Do not put the Lord your God to the test." Again, the devil took him to a very high mountain and showed him all the kingdoms of the world and their splendor. "All this I will give you," he said, "if you will bow down and worship me." Jesus said to him, "Away from me, Satan! For it is written: 'Worship the Lord your God, and serve him only." Then the devil left him, and angels came and attended him."

Matthew 4:1–11 (NIV)

• • •

In these passages, we learn that the servants of God who fasted forty days and forty nights did so to receive commandments with enlightenment and revelation, direction and strength for spiritual journeys, and power to overcome temptation. Because of their fasting, they were given the opportunities to prove the power and authority of God's Word against Satan's attacks.

In all four references of forty days and nights of prayer

and fasting, the servants of God were in God's presence the entire time. Two references are to Moses, one to Elijah, and one to Jesus, the Son of God. In the accounts of Moses, Elijah, and Jesus, the host of heaven ministered to each. Moses was ministered to by God himself the entire forty days and forty nights, Elijah was ministered to by the Angel of the Lord, and Jesus was ministered to by the Spirit through the entire forty days and forty nights, and angels from heaven ministered to him at the end of the forty days and forty nights. When you take on an endeavor such as fasting, rest assured that God will not leave you alone. While you are exercising the discipline of denying your flesh, God will strengthen you with a strong sense of his presence. While Moses was fasting on Mount Sinai, God was having conversation with him, giving him the law, and expressing his displeasure with the sin of the people. Daniel, Shadrach, Meshach, and Abednego started their fasting while in their roles as eunuchs in Babylon, and they practiced fasting at other times as well. When Nebuchadnezzar had Shadrach, Meshach, and Abednego cast into the fiery furnace, he witnessed the Son of God walking in the fire with them, protecting them from the flames. Nebuchadnezzar also had Daniel thrown into the den of lions; the angel of the Lord was with him all night to deliver him from the lions so no harm would come upon him. Be encouraged that denying the flesh by fasting develops a relationship with God that when found in trials and persecution, the Lord will protect and deliver you through your difficult times. Favor with man and God is another benefit that comes through fasting, which Daniel received from the king that also fasted all night on his behalf.

This 40-day prayer and fasting guide was designed with scripture that will assist you to stay in the presence of God, receive revelation, know your calling with direction, and prove the power and authority of the Word of God in overcoming Satan's temptations.

While using this guide, your study time will be divided into five sections, each with scripture to focus your prayer and to study the specific areas. The sections are divided as follows:

1. The Presence of God

2. Revelation and Enlightenment

3. Your Calling, Election, and Direction

4. Temptation and Trials

5. Power and Authority

Being in the presence of God is evidence that we are his children, and he is our Father. The Lord being with us in every area of our lives at all times, is also evidence of his unwavering faithfulness. Working to constantly recognize the presence of God in our lives will bring enlightenment, direction in our calling, a desire to overcome temptation, and a deeper revelation of our authority in Christ. The promises of God on his part are never to be doubted. Whether we are on the mountain or struggling in the valley, God is with us, because he cannot lie (Titus 1:2). We must believe that God exists and that he rewards those who earnestly seek him (Hebrews 11:6). With this in mind, while in the darkest valley, we must seek him, and we will find that he hasn't gone anywhere. Trusting what he has said will always see us through whether we feel his presence or not. It's by faith, not by works or feelings. It is a great blessing to know that we are in the presence of our God at all times and under all circumstances. Never allow the lie of loneliness to cause you to doubt that a single set of footprints in the sand of life are yours and not God's! Study each scripture below and know there is nothing you do that isn't done in the presence of the Lord!

Apply to your life the revelations you receive from the following scriptures during your prayer and fasting period.

• • •

You can eat your meals in the presence of the Lord.

Exodus 18:12 (NIV)

Then Jethro, Moses' father-in-law, brought a burnt offering and other sacrifices to God, and Aaron came with all the elders of Israel to *eat bread* with Moses' father-in-law *in the presence of God.*

• • •

Rejoice in all your work in the presence of the Lord.

Deuteronomy 12:18 (NIV)

Instead, you are to eat them in the presence of the LORD your God at the place the LORD your God will choose—you, your sons and daughters, your menservants and maidservants, and the Levites from your towns—and you are to *rejoice before the* LORD *your God in everything you put your hand to.*

• • •

Pray in the presence of the Lord.

1 Kings 18:28 (NIV)

Yet give attention to your servant's prayer and his plea for mercy, O LORD my God. *Hear the cry and the prayer that your servant is praying in your presence this day.*

• • •

You can cry in the presence of the Lord.

2 Chronicles 34:27 (NIV)

Because your heart was responsive and you humbled yourself before God when you heard what he spoke against this place and its people, and *because you humbled yourself before me and tore your robes and wept in my presence,* I have heard you, declares the LORD.

• • •

Attend church and study in the presence of the Lord.

Acts 10:33 (NIV)

So I sent for you immediately, and it was good of you to come. Now *we are all here in the presence of*

God to listen to everything the Lord has commanded you to tell us.

• • •

You can rejoice in the presence of the Lord because of family and friends.

1 Thessalonians 3:9 (NIV)

How can we thank God enough for you in return for all the *joy* we have *in the presence of our God because of you?*

The Presence of God

The Scripture for the next six days will focus on the presence of God. The most effective prayer warrior is one that remains in the presence of God by faith. There are times when you may feel that God is far away from you, and you may think your prayers are hindered because of it. This is the time when you must trust him and not rely on your feelings. God is faithful and he has promised to never leave or forsake you (Hebrews 13:5). Rest assured, God does hear, and he is very near! As near as the mention of his name!

The Presence of God
Day 1

Month	**Day**

Prayed ☐   Fasted ☐   Read & Prayed Scripture ☐

☐ Genesis 3:8 (NIV)

Then the man and his wife heard the sound of the LORD God as he was walking in the garden in the cool of the day, and they hid from the LORD God among the trees of the garden.

☐ Genesis 5:24 (NASB)

Enoch walked with God; and he was not, for God took him.

☐ Genesis 6:9 (AMP)

This is the history of the generations of Noah. Noah was a just and righteous man, blameless in his [evil] generation; Noah walked [in habitual fellowship] with God.

☐ Genesis 48:21 (NKJV)

Then Israel said to Joseph, "Behold, I am dying, but God will be with you and bring you back to the land of your fathers.

☐ Exodus 33:12–17 (NIV)

Moses said to the LORD, "You have been telling me, 'Lead these people,' but you have not let me know whom you will send with me. You have said, 'I know you by name and you have found favor with me.' If you are pleased with me, teach me your ways so I may know you and continue to find favor with you. Remember that this nation is your people." The LORD replied, "My Presence will go with you, and I will give you rest." Then Moses said to him, "If your Presence does not go with us, do not send us up from here. How will anyone know that you are pleased with me and with your people unless you go with us? What else will distinguish me and your people from all the other people on the face of the earth?" And the LORD said to Moses, "I will do the very thing you have asked, because I am pleased with you and I know you by name."

_____

_____

_____

_____

On the lines above, write revelations received, commitments / vows made, sins revealed and repented of, life directions received, callings / gifts / talents discovered, etc.

The Presence of God
Day 2

_____   _____
Month   **Day**

Prayed ☐   Fasted ☐   Read & Prayed Scripture ☐

☐ Exodus 34:9 (NIV)

"O Lord, if I have found favor in your eyes," he said, "then let the Lord go with us. Although this is a stiff-necked people, forgive our wickedness and our sin, and take us as your inheritance."

☐ 1 Chronicles 16:22–35 (NASB)

"Do not touch My anointed ones, And do My prophets no harm." Sing to the LORD, all the earth; Proclaim good tidings of His salvation from day to day. Tell of His glory among the nations, His wonderful deeds among all the peoples. For great is the LORD, and greatly to be praised; He also is to be feared above all gods. For all the gods of the peoples are idols, But the LORD made the heavens. Splendor and majesty are before Him, Strength and joy are in His place. Ascribe to the LORD, O families of the peoples, Ascribe to the LORD glory and strength. Ascribe to the LORD the glory due His name; Bring an offering, and come before Him; Worship the

LORD in holy array. Tremble before Him, all the earth; Indeed, the world is firmly established, it will not be moved. Let the heavens be glad, and let the earth rejoice; And let them say among the nations, "The LORD reigns." Let the sea roar, and all it contains; Let the field exult, and all that is in it. Then the trees of the forest will sing for joy before the LORD; For He is coming to judge the earth. O give thanks to the LORD, for He is good; For His lovingkindness is everlasting. Then say, "Save us, O God of our salvation, And gather us and deliver us from the nations, To give thanks to Your holy name, And glory in Your praise."

☐ 2 Chronicles 20:15, 17 (AMP)

He said, Hearken, all Judah, you inhabitants of Jerusalem, and you King Jehoshaphat. The Lord says this to you: Be not afraid or dismayed at this great multitude; for the battle is not yours, but God's...You shall not need to fight in this battle; take your positions, stand still, and see the deliverance of the Lord [Who is] with you, O Judah and Jerusalem. Fear not nor be dismayed. Tomorrow go out against them, for the Lord is with you.

_____

On the lines above, write revelations received, commitments / vows made, sins revealed and repented of, life directions received, callings / gifts / talents discovered, etc.

The Presence of God
Day 3

_____   _____
Month   **Day**

Prayed ☐   Fasted ☐   Read & Prayed Scripture ☐

☐ Job 1:12 (NIV)

The LORD said to Satan, "Very well, then, everything he has is in your hands, but on the man himself do not lay a finger." Then Satan went out from the presence of the LORD.

☐ Psalm 16:11 (NASB)

You will make known to me the path of life; In Your presence is fullness of joy; In Your right hand there are pleasures forever.

☐ Psalm 17:2 (AMP)

Let my sentence of vindication come from You! May Your eyes behold the things that are just and upright.

☐ Psalm 31:19–20 (NKJV)

Oh, how great is Your goodness, Which You have laid up for those who fear You, Which You have prepared for those who trust in You In the presence of the sons of men! You shall hide them in the secret place of Your presence From the plots of man; You shall keep them secretly in a pavilion From the strife of tongues.

☐ Psalm 51:10–11 (NIV)

Create in me a pure heart, O God, and renew a steadfast spirit within me. Do not cast me from your presence or take your Holy Spirit from me.

☐ Psalm 91:1–2 (NASB)

He who dwells in the shelter of the Most High will abide in the shadow of the Almighty. I will say to the LORD, "My refuge and my fortress, My God, in whom I trust!"

☐ Psalm 91:9–10 (AMP)

Because you have made the Lord your refuge, and the Most High your dwelling place. There shall no evil befall you, nor any plague or calamity come near your tent.

_____

_____

_____

_____

On the lines above, write revelations received, commitments / vows made, sins revealed and repented of, life directions, callings / gifts / talents discovered, etc.

The Presence of God
Day 4

_____   _____
              Month   **Day**

Prayed ☐   Fasted ☐   Read & Prayed Scripture ☐

☐ Psalm 95:2 (NIV)

Let us come before him with thanksgiving and extol him with music and song.

☐ Psalm 100:2 (NASB)

Serve the LORD with gladness; Come before Him with joyful singing.

☐ Psalm 139:7 (AMP)

Where could I go from Your Spirit? Or where could I flee from Your presence?

☐ Psalm 140:13 (NKJV)

Surely the righteous shall give thanks to Your name; The upright shall dwell in Your presence.

☐ Isaiah 1:18 (NIV)

"Come now, let us reason together," says the LORD. "Though your sins are like scarlet, they shall be as white as snow; though they are red as crimson, they shall be like wool.

☐ Isaiah 6:1–5 (NASB)

In the year of King Uzziah's death I saw the Lord sitting on a throne, lofty and exalted, with the train of His robe filling the temple. Seraphim stood above Him, each having six wings: with two he covered his face, and with two he covered his feet, and with two he flew. And one called out to another and said, "Holy, Holy, Holy, is the LORD of hosts, The whole earth is full of His glory." And the foundations of the thresholds trembled at the voice of him who called out, while the temple was filling with smoke. Then I said, "Woe is me, for I am ruined! Because I am a man of unclean lips, And I live among a people of unclean lips; For my eyes have seen the King, the LORD of hosts."

☐ Isaiah 55:6 (AMP)

Seek, inquire for, and require the Lord while He may be found [claiming Him by necessity and by right]; call upon Him while He is near.

_____

_____

_____

_____

On the lines above, write revelations received, commitments / vows made, sins revealed and repented of, life directions, callings / gifts / talents discovered, etc.

The Presence of God
Day 5

Month   **Day**

Prayed ☐   Fasted ☐   Read & Prayed Scripture ☐

☐ Amos 5:14 (NIV)

Seek good, not evil, that you may live. Then the LORD God Almighty will be with you, just as you say he is.

☐ Jonah 1:3 (NASB)

But Jonah rose up to flee to Tarshish from the presence of the LORD So he went down to Joppa, found a ship which was going to Tarshish, paid the fare and went down into it to go with them to Tarshish from the presence of the LORD.

☐ Zephaniah 1:7 (AMP)

[Hush!] Be silent before the Lord God, for the day [of the vengeance] of the Lord is near; for the Lord has prepared a sacrifice, and He has set apart [for His use] those who have accepted His invitation.

☐ Matthew 18:20 (NKJV)

For where two or three are gathered together in My name, I am there in the midst of them.

☐ Matthew 28:20 (NIV)

And teaching them to obey everything I have commanded you. And surely I am with you always, to the very end of the age.

☐ John 20:19 (NASB)

So when it was evening on that day, the first day of the week, and when the doors were shut where the disciples were, for fear of the Jews, Jesus came and stood in their midst and said to them, "Peace be with you."

☐ Acts 3:19 (AMP)

So repent (change your mind and purpose); turn around and return [to God], that your sins may be erased (blotted out, wiped clean), that times of refreshing (of recovering from the effects of heat, of reviving with fresh air) may come from the presence of the Lord....

_____

_____

_____

_____

On the lines above, write revelations received, commitments / vows made, sins revealed and repented of, life directions, callings / gifts / talents discovered, etc.

The Presence of God
Day 6

-----------------------   ------------------------

Month   *Day*

Prayed ☐   Fasted ☐   Read & Prayed Scripture ☐

☐ 1 Corinthians 1:29 (NIV)

So that no one may boast before him.

☐ 2 Corinthians 13:11 (NASB)

Finally, brethren, rejoice, be made complete, be comforted, be like-minded, live in peace; and the God of love and peace will be with you.

☐ 1 Thessalonians 2:19 (AMP)

For what is our hope or happiness or our victor's wreath of exultant triumph when we stand in the presence of our Lord Jesus at His coming? Is it not you?

☐ Hebrews 13:5 (NKJV)

Let your conduct be without covetousness; be content with such things as you have. For He Himself has said, "I will never leave you nor forsake you."

☐ Jude 1:24 (NIV)

To him who is able to keep you from falling

and to present you before his glorious presence without fault and with great joy...

☐ Revelation 2:1 (NASB)

To the angel of the church in Ephesus write: The One who holds the seven stars in His right hand, the One who walks among the seven golden lampstands, says this....

☐ Revelation 15:8 (AMP)

And the sanctuary was filled with smoke from the glory (the radiance, the splendor) of God and from His might and power, and no one was able to go into the sanctuary until the seven plagues (afflictions, calamities) of the seven angels were ended.

☐ Revelation 21:23 (NKJV)

The city had no need of the sun or of the moon to shine in it, for the glory of God illuminated it. The Lamb is its light.

_____

_____

_____

_____

On the lines above, write revelations received, commitments / vows made, sins revealed and repented of, life directions, callings / gifts / talents discovered, etc.

Revelation & Enlightenment

The Scripture for the next ten days will focus on revelation and enlightenment, which can be received from God through his Word, dreams and visions, gifts of the Holy Ghost, life's experiences, and other saints. Much knowledge has been gained because God has revealed secrets unto men from the beginning. These secrets have been in the form of spiritual and secular knowledge. When a person is enlightened or receives revelation from his or her experiences, whether through mistakes, failures, or research (seeking), they receive knowledge. This is the reason there have been so many great men and women who have spread the Word of God all over the world and have had great breakthroughs in the technological and medical fields for the good of mankind. Wisdom is a great quality that comes as more knowledge is obtained. As our spiritual knowledge is increased, we become like spiritual giants in our faith. Praise God, honor him by being faithful, and committed in your servitude to him with the revelations you have received. You must also share that knowledge with others, realizing that God enlightens us to gain strength for unity with other Children of God, and to comfort and encourage one another. Remember, knowledge not used is knowledge abused.

Revelation and Enlightenment
Day 7

Month	**Day**

Prayed ☐   Fasted ☐   Read & Prayed Scripture ☐

☐ Genesis 22:11–18 (NIV)

But the angel of the LORD called out to him from heaven, "Abraham! Abraham!" "Here I am," he replied. "Do not lay a hand on the boy," he said. "Do not do anything to him. Now I know that you fear God, because you have not withheld from me your son, your only son." Abraham looked up and there in a thicket he saw a ram caught by its horns. He went over and took the ram and sacrificed it as a burnt offering instead of his son. So Abraham called that place The LORD Will Provide. And to this day it is said, "On the mountain of the LORD it will be provided." The angel of the LORD called to Abraham from heaven a second time and said, "I swear by myself, declares the LORD, that because you have done this and have not withheld your son, your only son, I will surely bless you and make your descendants as numerous as the stars in the sky and as the sand on the seashore. Your descendants will take possession of the cities of their enemies, and through your offspring all nations on earth will be blessed, because you have obeyed me."

☐ Exodus 18:19–24 (NASB)

"Now listen to me: I will give you counsel, and God be with you. You be the people's representative before God, and you bring the disputes to God, then teach them the statutes and the laws, and make known to them the way in which they are to walk and the work they are to do. "Furthermore, you shall select out of all the people able men who fear God, men of truth, those who hate dishonest gain; and you shall place these over them as leaders of thousands, of hundreds, of fifties and of tens. "Let them judge the people at all times; and let it be that every major dispute they will bring to you, but every minor dispute they themselves will judge So it will be easier for you, and they will bear the burden with you. "If you do this thing and God so commands you, then you will be able to endure, and all these people also will go to their place in peace." So Moses listened to his father-in-law and did all that he had said.

_____

_____

_____

_____

On the lines above, write revelations received, commitments / vows made, sins revealed and repented of, life directions, callings / gifts / talents discovered, etc.

Revelation and Enlightenment
Day 8

_____   _____
Month   *Day*

Prayed ☐   Fasted ☐   Read & Prayed Scripture ☐

☐   Numbers 22:22–33 (NIV)

But God was very angry when he went, and the
angel of the LORD stood in the road to oppose
him. Balaam was riding on his donkey, and his
two servants were with him. When the donkey
saw the angel of the LORD standing in the road
with a drawn sword in his hand, she turned off
the road into a field. Balaam beat her to get her
back on the road. Then the angel of the LORD
stood in a narrow path between two vineyards,
with walls on both sides. When the donkey saw
the angel of the LORD, she pressed close to the
wall, crushing Balaam's foot against it. So he beat
her again. Then the angel of the LORD moved on
ahead and stood in a narrow place where there
was no room to turn, either to the right or to
the left. When the donkey saw the angel of the
LORD, she lay down under Balaam, and he was
angry and beat her with his staff. Then the LORD
opened the donkey's mouth, and she said to

Balaam, "What have I done to you to make you beat me these three times?" Balaam answered the donkey, "You have made a fool of me! If I had a sword in my hand, I would kill you right now." The donkey said to Balaam, "Am I not your own donkey, which you have always ridden, to this day? Have I been in the habit of doing this to you?" "No," he said. Then the LORD opened Balaam's eyes, and he saw the angel of the LORD standing in the road with his sword drawn. So he bowed low and fell facedown. The angel of the LORD asked him, "Why have you beaten your donkey these three times? I have come here to oppose you because your path is a reckless one before me. The donkey saw me and turned away from me these three times. If she had not turned away, I would certainly have killed you by now, but I would have spared her."

☐ Deuteronomy 29:29 (NASB)

The secret things belong to the LORD our God, but the things revealed belong to us and to our sons forever, that we may observe all the words of this law.

_____

_____

_____

On the lines above, write revelations received, commitments / vows made, sins revealed and repented of, life directions, callings / gifts / talents discovered, etc.

Revelation and Enlightenment
Day 9

Month   **Day**

Prayed ☐   Fasted ☐   Read & Prayed Scripture ☐

☐   1 Samuel 3:7, 21 (NIV)

Now Samuel did not yet know the LORD: The word of the LORD had not yet been revealed to him....The LORD continued to appear at Shiloh, and there he revealed himself to Samuel through his word.

☐   2 Kings 6:15–17 (NASB)

Now when the attendant of the man of God had risen early and gone out, behold, an army with horses and chariots was circling the city. And his servant said to him, "Alas, my master! What shall we do?" So he answered, "Do not fear, for those who are with us are more than those who are with them." Then Elisha prayed and said, "O LORD, I pray, open his eyes that he may see " And the LORD opened the servant's eyes and he saw; and behold, the mountain was full of horses and chariots of fire all around Elisha.

☐   2 Chronicles 26:5 (AMP)

He set himself to seek God in the days of

Zechariah, who instructed him in the things of God; and as long as he sought (inquired of, yearned for) the Lord, God made him prosper.

☐ Psalm 18:28 (NKJV)

For You will light my lamp; The LORD my God will enlighten my darkness.

☐ Psalm 19:8 (NIV)

The precepts of the LORD are right, giving joy to the heart. The commands of the LORD are radiant, giving light to the eyes.

☐ Isaiah 40:5 (NASB)

Then the glory of the LORD will be revealed, And all flesh will see it together; For the mouth of the LORD has spoken."

_____

_____

_____

_____

On the lines above, write revelations received, commitments / vows made, sins revealed and repented of, life directions, callings / gifts / talents discovered, etc.

Revelation and Enlightenment
Day 10

| **Month** | | **Day** |

Prayed ☐   Fasted ☐   Read & Prayed Scripture ☐

☐ Isaiah 56:1 (NIV)

This is what the LORD says: "Maintain justice and do what is right, for my salvation is close at hand and my righteousness will soon be revealed.

☐ Jeremiah 33:6 (NASB)

'Behold, I will bring to it health and healing, and I will heal them; and I will reveal to them an abundance of peace and truth.

☐ Daniel 1:17 (AMP)

As for these four youths, God gave them knowledge and skill in all learning and wisdom, and Daniel had understanding in all [kinds of] visions and dreams.

☐ Daniel 2:19 (NKJV)

Then the secret was revealed to Daniel in a night vision. So Daniel blessed the God of heaven.

☐ Daniel 2:22 (NIV)

He reveals deep and hidden things; he knows what lies in darkness, and light dwells with him.

☐ Daniel 2:28–30 (NASB)

"However, there is a God in heaven who reveals mysteries, and He has made known to King Nebuchadnezzar what will take place in the latter days This was your dream and the visions in your mind while on your bed. "As for you, O king, while on your bed your thoughts turned to what would take place in the future; and He who reveals mysteries has made known to you what will take place. "But as for me, this mystery has not been revealed to me for any wisdom residing in me more than in any other living man, but for the purpose of making the interpretation known to the king, and that you may understand the thoughts of your mind.

On the lines above, write revelations received, commitments / vows made, sins revealed and repented of, life directions, callings / gifts / talents discovered, etc.

Revelation and Enlightenment
Day 11

Month	**Day**

Prayed ☐   Fasted ☐   Read & Prayed Scripture ☐

☐ Amos 3:7 (NIV)

Surely the Sovereign LORD does nothing without revealing his plan to his servants the prophets.

☐ Matthew 10:26 (NASB)

"Therefore do not fear them, for there is nothing concealed that will not be revealed, or hidden that will not be known.

☐ Matthew 11:25 (AMP)

At that time Jesus began to say, I thank You, Father, Lord of heaven and earth [and] I acknowledge openly and joyfully to Your honor, that You have hidden these things from the wise and clever and learned, and revealed them to babies [to the childish, untaught, and unskilled].

☐ Matthew 16:13–17 (NKJV)

When Jesus came into the region of Caesarea Philippi, He asked His disciples, saying, "Who do men say that I, the Son of Man, am?" So they said, "Some say John the Baptist, some Elijah, and others Jeremiah or one of the prophets." He said to them, "But who do you say that I am?" Simon Peter answered and said, "You are the Christ, the Son of the living God." Jesus answered and said to him, "Blessed are you, Simon Bar-Jonah, for flesh and blood has not revealed this to you, but My Father who is in heaven.

☐ Matthew 16:27 (NIV)

For the Son of Man is going to come in his Father's glory with his angels, and then he will reward each person according to what he has done.

☐ Luke 10:21 (NASB)

At that very time He rejoiced greatly in the Holy Spirit, and said, "I praise You, O Father, Lord of heaven and earth, that You have hidden these things from the wise and intelligent and have revealed them to infants. Yes, Father, for this way was well-pleasing in Your sight.

_____

_____

_____

_____

On the lines above, write revelations received, commitments / vows made, sins revealed and repented of, life directions, callings / gifts / talents discovered, etc.

Revelation and Enlightenment
Day 12

Month	Day

Prayed ☐ Fasted ☐ Read & Prayed Scripture ☐

☐ Acts 7:55–56 (NIV)

But Stephen, full of the Holy Spirit, looked up to heaven and saw the glory of God, and Jesus standing at the right hand of God. "Look," he said, "I see heaven open and the Son of Man standing at the right hand of God."

☐ Acts 27:22–24 (NASB)

"Yet now I urge you to keep up your courage, for there will be no loss of life among you, but only of the ship. "For this very night an angel of the God to whom I belong and whom I serve stood before me, saying, 'Do not be afraid, Paul; you must stand before Caesar; and behold, God has granted you all those who are sailing with you.'

☐ Romans 1:17 (AMP)

For in the Gospel a righteousness which God ascribes is revealed, both springing from faith and leading to faith [disclosed through the way of faith that arouses to more faith]. As it is written, The man who through faith is just and upright shall live and shall live by faith.

☐ Romans 2:3–5 (NKJV)

And do you think this, O man, you who judge those practicing such things, and doing the same, that you will escape the judgment of God? Or do you despise the riches of His goodness, forbearance, and longsuffering, not knowing that the goodness of God leads you to repentance? But in accordance with your hardness and your impenitent heart you are treasuring up for yourself wrath in the day of wrath and revelation of the righteous judgment of God....

☐ Romans 16:25–26 (NIV)

Now to him who is able to establish you by my gospel and the proclamation of Jesus Christ, according to the revelation of the mystery hidden for long ages past, but now revealed and made known through the prophetic writings by the command of the eternal God, so that all nations might believe and obey him....

_____

_____

_____

_____

On the lines above, write revelations received, commitments / vows made, sins revealed and repented of, life directions, callings / gifts / talents discovered, etc.

Revelation and Enlightenment
Day 13

__Month__	__Day__

Prayed ☐   Fasted ☐   Read & Prayed Scripture ☐

☐ 1 Corinthians 2:10 (NIV)

But God has revealed it to us by his Spirit. The Spirit searches all things, even the deep things of God.

☐ 1 Corinthians 14:6 (NASB)

But now, brethren, if I come to you speaking in tongues, what will I profit you unless I speak to you either by way of revelation or of knowledge or of prophecy or of teaching?

☐ 2 Corinthians 12:1 (AMP)

TRUE, THERE is nothing to be gained by it, but [as I am obliged] to boast, I will go on to visions and revelations of the Lord.

☐ 2 Corinthians 12:7–10 (NKJV)

And lest I should be exalted above measure by the abundance of the revelations, a thorn in the flesh was given to me, a messenger of Satan to buffet me, lest I be exalted above measure. Concerning this thing I pleaded with the Lord three times that it might depart from me. And He said to me, "My grace is sufficient for you, for My strength is made perfect in weakness." Therefore most gladly I will rather boast in my infirmities, that the power of Christ may rest upon me. Therefore I take pleasure in infirmities, in reproaches, in needs, in persecutions, in distresses, for Christ's sake. For when I am weak, then I am strong.

☐ Galatians 1:12 (NIV)

I did not receive it from any man, nor was I taught it; rather, I received it by revelation from Jesus Christ.

☐ Galatians 1:16 (NASB)

To reveal His Son in me so that I might preach Him among the Gentiles, I did not immediately consult with flesh and blood....

_____

_____

_____

_____

On the lines above, write revelations received, commitments / vows made, sins revealed and repented of, life directions, callings / gifts / talents discovered, etc.

Revelation and Enlightenment
Day 14

Month	Day

Prayed ☐   Fasted ☐   Read & Prayed Scripture ☐

☐ Galatians 2:2 (NIV)

I went in response to a revelation and set before them the gospel that I preach among the Gentiles. But I did this privately to those who seemed to be leaders, for fear that I was running or had run my race in vain.

☐ 2 Corinthians 12:1–4 (NASB)

Boasting is necessary, though it is not profitable; but I will go on to visions and revelations of the Lord. I know a man in Christ who fourteen years ago—whether in the body I do not know, or out of the body I do not know, God knows—such a man was caught up to the third heaven. And I know how such a man—whether in the body or apart from the body I do not know, God knows—was caught up into Paradise and heard inexpressible words, which a man is not permitted to speak.

☐ 2 Corinthians 12:7 (AMP)

And to keep me from being puffed up and too much elated by the exceeding greatness (preeminence) of these revelations, there was given me a thorn (a splinter) in the flesh, a messenger of Satan, to rack and buffet and harass me, to keep me from being excessively exalted.

☐ Ephesians 1:17–23 (NKJV)

That the God of our Lord Jesus Christ, the Father of glory, may give to you the spirit of wisdom and revelation in the knowledge of Him, the eyes of your understanding being enlightened; that you may know what is the hope of His calling, what are the riches of the glory of His inheritance in the saints, and what is the exceeding greatness of His power toward us who believe, according to the working of His mighty power which He worked in Christ when He raised Him from the dead and seated Him at His right hand in the heavenly places, far above all principality and power and might and dominion, and every name that is named, not only in this age but also in that which is to come. And He put all things under His feet, and gave Him to be head over all things to the church, which is His body, the fullness of Him who fills all in all.

_____

_____

_____

On the lines above, write revelations received, commitments / vows made, sins revealed and repented of, life directions, callings / gifts / talents discovered, etc.

Revelation and Enlightenment
Day 15

Month	Day

Prayed ☐   Fasted ☐   Read & Prayed Scripture ☐

☐   Ephesians 3:2–7 (NIV)

Surely you have heard about the administration of God's grace that was given to me for you, that is, the mystery made known to me by revelation, as I have already written briefly. In reading this, then, you will be able to understand my insight into the mystery of Christ, which was not made known to men in other generations as it has now been revealed by the Spirit to God's holy apostles and prophets. This mystery is that through the gospel the Gentiles are heirs together with Israel, members together of one body, and sharers together in the promise in Christ Jesus. I became a servant of this gospel by the gift of God's grace given me through the working of his power.

☐   Philippians 3:13–15 (NASB)

Brethren, I do not regard myself as having laid hold of it yet; but one thing I do: forgetting what lies behind and reaching forward to what lies ahead, I press on toward the goal for the prize of the upward call of God in Christ Jesus. Let us therefore, as many as are perfect, have this attitude; and if in anything you have a different attitude, God will reveal that also to you....

☐ 2 Timothy 3:16–17 (AMP)

Every Scripture is God-breathed (given by His inspiration) and profitable for instruction, for reproof and conviction of sin, for correction of error and discipline in obedience, [and] for training in righteousness (in holy living, in conformity to God's will in thought, purpose, and action), So that the man of God may be complete and proficient, well fitted and thoroughly equipped for every good work.

☐ Hebrews 6:4–6 (NKJV)

For it is impossible for those who were once enlightened, and have tasted the heavenly gift, and have become partakers of the Holy Spirit, and have tasted the good word of God and the powers of the age to come, if they fall away, to renew them again to repentance, since they crucify again for themselves the Son of God, and put Him to an open shame.

_____

_____

_____

On the lines above, write revelations received, commitments / vows made, sins revealed and repented of, life directions, callings / gifts / talents discovered, etc.

Revelation and Enlightenment
Day 16

Month	Day

Prayed ☐   Fasted ☐   Read & Prayed Scripture ☐

☐ James 4:13–17 (NIV)

Now listen, you who say, "Today or tomorrow we will go to this or that city, spend a year there, carry on business and make money." Why, you do not even know what will happen tomorrow. What is your life? You are a mist that appears for a little while and then vanishes. Instead, you ought to say, "If it is the Lord's will, we will live and do this or that." As it is, you boast and brag. All such boasting is evil. Anyone, then, who knows the good he ought to do and doesn't do it, sins.

☐ 1 Peter 4:13 (NASB)

But to the degree that you share the sufferings of Christ, keep on rejoicing, so that also at the revelation of His glory you may rejoice with exultation.

☐ 2 Peter 1:20–21 (AMP)

[Yet] first [you must] understand this, that no prophecy of Scripture is [a matter] of any personal or private or special interpretation (loosening, solving). For no prophecy ever originated because some man willed it [to do so—it never came by human impulse], but men spoke from God who were borne along (moved and impelled) by the Holy Spirit.

☐ 1 John 5:11–13 (NKJV)

And this is the testimony: that God has given us eternal life, and this life is in His Son. He who has the Son has life; he who does not have the Son of God does not have life. These things I have written to you who believe in the name of the Son of God, that you may know that you have eternal life, and that you may continue to believe in the name of the Son of God.

☐ Revelation 1:1–3 (NIV)

The revelation of Jesus Christ, which God gave him to show his servants what must soon take place. He made it known by sending his angel to his servant John, who testifies to everything he saw—that is, the word of God and the testimony of Jesus Christ. Blessed is the one who reads the words of this prophecy, and blessed are those who hear it and take to heart what is written in it, because the time is near.

_____

_____

_____

_____

On the lines above, write revelations received, commitments / vows made, sins revealed and repented of, life directions, callings / gifts / talents discovered, etc.

Your Calling, Election,
& Direction

The Scripture for the next ten days will focus on your calling, election, and direction. We need to be sure of our calling and election by trusting that God has called us for a purpose and then yield to his desires for us. Also, we should seek God for his direction for our lives. If God has called us, he can surely direct us. Many people do not know their purpose or how to proceed with their calling, much less which way to go. God has life's answers when we pray and then listen patiently for him to speak to us. We cannot fulfill God's will without knowing his will. The only way to know God's will is to ask him. If God calls you to it, he will surely see you through it. The Lord has ordered our steps and he will lead us in them.

Your Calling, Election, and Direction
Day 17

| ***Month*** | ***Day*** |

Prayed ☐   Fasted ☐   Read & Prayed Scripture ☐

☐ Genesis 2:15 (NIV)

The Lord God took the man and put him in the Garden of Eden to work it and take care of it.

☐ Genesis 6:13–14 (NASB)

Then God said to Noah, "The end of all flesh has come before Me; for the earth is filled with violence because of them; and behold, I am about to destroy them with the earth. "Make for yourself an ark of gopher wood; you shall make the ark with rooms, and shall cover it inside and out with pitch.

☐ Genesis 7:1–2 (AMP)

AND THE Lord said to Noah, Come with all your household into the ark, for I have seen you to be righteous (upright and in right standing) before Me in this generation. Of every clean beast you shall receive and take with you seven pairs, the male and his mate, and of beasts that are not clean a pair of each kind, the male and his mate....

☐ Genesis 8:15–17 (NKJV)

Then God spoke to Noah, saying, "Go out of the ark, you and your wife, and your sons and your sons' wives with you. Bring out with you every living thing of all flesh that is with you: birds and cattle and every creeping thing that creeps on the earth, so that they may abound on the earth, and be fruitful and multiply on the earth."

☐ Genesis 12:1–2 (NIV)

The LORD had said to Abram, "Leave your country, your people and your father's household and go to the land I will show you. "I will make you into a great nation and I will bless you; I will make your name great, and you will be a blessing.

☐ Genesis 17:19 (NASB)

But God said, "No, but Sarah your wife will bear you a son, and you shall call his name Isaac; and I will establish My covenant with him for an everlasting covenant for his descendants after him.

_____

_____

_____

_____

On the lines above, write revelations received, commitments / vows made, sins revealed and repented of, life directions, callings / gifts / talents discovered, etc.

Your Calling, Election, and Direction
Day 18

Month   ***Day***

Prayed ☐   Fasted ☐   Read & Prayed Scripture ☐

☐   Genesis 22:1–2, 9–12 (NIV)

Some time later God tested Abraham. He said to him, "Abraham!" "Here I am," he replied. Then God said, "Take your son, your only son, Isaac, whom you love, and go to the region of Moriah. Sacrifice him there as a burnt offering on one of the mountains I will tell you about."…When they reached the place God had told him about, Abraham built an altar there and arranged the wood on it. He bound his son Isaac and laid him on the altar, on top of the wood. Then he reached out his hand and took the knife to slay his son. But the angel of the LORD called out to him from heaven, "Abraham! Abraham!" "Here I am," he replied. "Do not lay a hand on the boy," he said. "Do not do anything to him. Now I know that you fear God, because you have not withheld from me your son, your only son."

☐   Genesis 24:12, 14–19, 27 (NASB)

He said, "O LORD, the God of my master

Abraham, please grant me success today, and show lovingkindness to my master Abraham... Now may it be that the girl to whom I say, 'Please let down your jar so that I may drink,' and who answers, 'Drink, and I will water your camels also'—may she be the one whom You have appointed for Your servant Isaac; and by this I will know that You have shown lovingkindness to my master." Before he had finished speaking, behold, Rebekah who was born to Bethuel the son of Milcah, the wife of Abraham's brother Nahor, came out with her jar on her shoulder. The girl was very beautiful, a virgin, and no man had had relations with her; and she went down to the spring and filled her jar and came up. Then the servant ran to meet her, and said, "Please let me drink a little water from your jar." She said, "Drink, my lord"; and she quickly lowered her jar to her hand, and gave him a drink. Now when she had finished giving him a drink, she said, "I will draw also for your camels until they have finished drinking."...He said, "Blessed be the LORD, the God of my master Abraham, who has not forsaken His lovingkindness and His truth toward my master; as for me, the LORD has guided me in the way to the house of my master's brothers."

_____

_____

_____

On the lines above, write revelations received, commitments / vows made, sins revealed and repented of, life directions, callings / gifts / talents discovered, etc.

Your Calling, Election, and Direction
Day 19

Month	*Day*

Prayed ☐   Fasted ☐   Read & Prayed Scripture ☐

☐ Genesis 26:2–3 (NIV)

The LORD appeared to Isaac and said, "Do not go down to Egypt; live in the land where I tell you to live. Stay in this land for a while, and I will be with you and will bless you. For to you and your descendants I will give all these lands and will confirm the oath I swore to your father Abraham.

☐ Genesis 28:10–15 (NASB)

Then Jacob departed from Beersheba and went toward Haran. He came to a certain place and spent the night there, because the sun had set; and he took one of the stones of the place and put it under his head, and lay down in that place. He had a dream, and behold, a ladder was set on the earth with its top reaching to heaven; and behold, the angels of God were ascending and descending on it. And behold, the LORD stood above it and said, "I am the LORD, the God of your father Abraham and the God of Isaac; the land on which you lie, I will give it to you and to your descendants. "Your descendants will also be like the dust of the earth, and you will spread out to the west and to the east and to the north and to the south; and in you and in your descendants shall all the families of the earth be blessed. "Behold, I am with you and will keep you wherever you go, and will bring you back to this land; for I will not leave you until I have done what I have promised you."

☐ Genesis 45:5 (AMP)

But now, do not be distressed and disheartened or vexed and angry with yourselves because you sold me here, for God sent me ahead of you to preserve life.

☐ Exodus 3:10 (NKJV)

Come now, therefore, and I will send you to Pharaoh that you may bring My people, the children of Israel, out of Egypt."

☐ Exodus 4:12 (NIV)

Now go; I will help you speak and will teach you what to say."

_____

_____

_____

On the lines above, write revelations received, commitments / vows made, sins revealed and repented of, life directions, callings / gifts / talents discovered, etc.

Your Calling, Election, and Direction
Day 20

_____   _____
Month   ***Day***

Prayed ☐   Fasted ☐   Read & Prayed Scripture ☐

☐ Judges 6:12–14 (NIV)

When the angel of the LORD appeared to Gideon,
he said, "The LORD is with you, mighty warrior."
"But sir," Gideon replied, "if the LORD is with us,
why has all this happened to us? Where are all his
wonders that our fathers told us about when they
said, 'Did not the LORD bring us up out of Egypt?'
But now the LORD has abandoned us and put us into
the hand of Midian." The LORD turned to him and
said, "Go in the strength you have and save Israel
out of Midian's hand. Am I not sending you?"

☐ 1 Samuel 16:11–13 (NASB)

And Samuel said to Jesse, "Are these all the
children?" And he said, "There remains yet the
youngest, and behold, he is tending the sheep."
Then Samuel said to Jesse, "Send and bring him;
for we will not sit down until he comes here." So
he sent and brought him in. Now he was ruddy,
with beautiful eyes and a handsome appearance
And the LORD said, " Arise, anoint him; for

this is he." Then Samuel took the horn of oil and anointed him in the midst of his brothers; and the Spirit of the LORD came mightily upon David from that day forward. And Samuel arose and went to Ramah.

☐ Psalm 37:23 (AMP)

The steps of a [good] man are directed and established by the Lord when He delights in his way [and He busies Himself with his every step].

☐ Proverbs 3:6 (NKJV)

In all your ways acknowledge Him, And He shall direct your paths.

☐ Proverbs 16:1, 9, 17 (NIV)

To man belong the plans of the heart, but from the LORD comes the reply of the tongue...In his heart a man plans his course, but the LORD determines his steps...The highway of the upright avoids evil; he who guards his way guards his life.

_____

_____

_____

_____

On the lines above, write revelations received, commitments / vows made, sins revealed and repented of, life directions, callings / gifts / talents discovered, etc.

Your Calling, Election, and Direction
Day 21

_____   _____
        Month   ***Day***

Prayed ☐   Fasted ☐   Read & Prayed Scripture ☐

☐ Isaiah 6:8 (NIV)

Then I heard the voice of the Lord saying, "Whom shall I send? And who will go for us?" And I said, "Here am I. Send me!"

☐ Isaiah 35:8 (NASB)

A highway will be there, a roadway, And it will be called the Highway of Holiness The unclean will not travel on it, But it will be for him who walks that way, And fools will not wander on it.

☐ Jeremiah 1:4–10 (AMP)

Then the word of the Lord came to me [Jeremiah], saying, Before I formed you in the womb I knew [and] approved of you [as My chosen instrument], and before you were born I separated and set you apart, consecrating you; [and] I appointed you as a prophet to the nations. Then said I, Ah, Lord God! Behold, I cannot speak, for I am only a youth. But the Lord said to me, Say not, I am only a youth; for you shall go to all to whom I shall send you, and whatever I command you, you shall speak. Be not afraid of them [their faces], for I am with you to deliver you, says the Lord. Then the Lord put forth His hand and touched my mouth. And the Lord said to me, Behold, I have put My words in your mouth. See, I have this day appointed you to the oversight of the nations and of the kingdoms to root out and pull down, to destroy and to overthrow, to build and to plant.

☐ Jeremiah 10:23 (NKJV)

O LORD, I know the way of man is not in himself; It is not in man who walks to direct his own steps.

☐ Ezekiel 2:3 (NIV)

He said: "Son of man, I am sending you to the Israelites, to a rebellious nation that has rebelled against me; they and their fathers have been in revolt against me to this very day.

_____

_____

_____

_____

On the lines above, write revelations received, commitments / vows made, sins revealed and repented of, life directions, callings / gifts / talents discovered, etc.

Your Calling, Election, and Direction
Day 22

Month	***Day***

Prayed ☐   Fasted ☐   Read & Prayed Scripture ☐

☐ Malachi 3:1 (NIV)

"See, I will send my messenger, who will prepare the way before me. Then suddenly the Lord you are seeking will come to his temple; the messenger of the covenant, whom you desire, will come," says the LORD Almighty.

☐ Malachi 4:5 (NASB)

"Behold, I am going to send you Elijah the prophet before the coming of the great and terrible day of the LORD.

☐ Matthew 2:12–14 (AMP)

And receiving an answer to their asking, they were divinely instructed and warned in a dream not to go back to Herod; so they departed to their own country by a different way. Now after they had gone, behold, an angel of the Lord appeared to Joseph in a dream and said, Get up! [Tenderly] take unto you the young Child and His mother and flee to Egypt; and remain there till I tell you [otherwise], for Herod intends to search for the

Child in order to destroy Him. And having risen, he took the Child and His mother by night and withdrew to Egypt...

☐ Matthew 7:13 (NKJV)

"Enter by the narrow gate; for wide is the gate and broad is the way that leads to destruction, and there are many who go in by it.

☐ Matthew 9:38 (NIV)

Ask the Lord of the harvest, therefore, to send out workers into his harvest field."

☐ Matthew 10:16–18 (NASB)

"Behold, I send you out as sheep in the midst of wolves; so be shrewd as serpents and innocent as doves. "But beware of men, for they will hand you over to the courts and scourge you in their synagogues; and you will even be brought before governors and kings for My sake, as a testimony to them and to the Gentiles.

_____

_____

_____

_____

On the lines above, write revelations received, commitments / vows made, sins revealed and repented of, life directions, callings / gifts / talents discovered, etc.

Your Calling, Election, and Direction
Day 23

Month	*Day*

Prayed ☐   Fasted ☐   Read & Prayed Scripture ☐

☐ Matthew 11:10 (NIV)

This is the one about whom it is written: "I will send my messenger ahead of you, who will prepare your way before you."

☐ Matthew 23:34 (NASB)

Therefore, behold, I am sending you prophets and wise men and scribes; some of them you will kill and crucify, and some of them you will scourge in your synagogues, and persecute from city to city....

☐ Matthew 28:5–8 (AMP)

But the angel said to the women, Do not be alarmed and frightened, for I know that you are looking for Jesus, Who was crucified. He is not here; He has risen, as He said [He would do]. Come, see the place where He lay. Then go quickly and tell His disciples, He has risen from the dead, and behold, He is going before you to Galilee; there you will see Him. Behold, I have told you. So they left the tomb hastily with fear and great joy and ran to tell the disciples.

☐ Mark 3:14 (NKJV)

Then He appointed twelve, that they might be with Him and that He might send them out to preach.

☐ Mark 5:18–20 (NIV)

As Jesus was getting into the boat, the man who had been demon-possessed begged to go with him. Jesus did not let him, but said, "Go home to your family and *tell* them how much the Lord has done for you, and how he has had mercy on you." So the man went away and began to tell in the Decapolis how much Jesus had done for him. And all the people were amazed.

☐ Mark 6:7 (NASB)

And He summoned the twelve and began to send them out in pairs, and gave them authority over the unclean spirits....

_____

_____

_____

_____

On the lines above, write revelations received, commitments / vows made, sins revealed and repented of, life directions, callings / gifts / talents discovered, etc.

Your Calling, Election, and Direction
Day 24

Month   ***Day***

Prayed ☐   Fasted ☐   Read & Prayed Scripture ☐

☐ Mark 16:15 (NIV)

He said to them, "Go into all the world and preach the good news to all creation.

☐ Luke 1:28–31 (NASB)

And coming in, he said to her, "Greetings, favored one! The Lord is with you." But she was very perplexed at this statement, and kept pondering what kind of salutation this was. The angel said to her, "Do not be afraid, Mary; for you have found favor with God. "And behold, you will conceive in your womb and bear a son, and you shall name Him Jesus.

☐ Luke 10:2–3 (AMP)

And He said to them, The harvest indeed is abundant there is much ripe grain], but the farmhands are few. Pray therefore the Lord of the harvest to send out laborers into His harvest. Go your way; behold, I send you out like lambs into the midst of wolves.

☐ Acts 7:34–36 (NKJV)

I have surely seen the oppression of My people who are in Egypt; I have heard their groaning and have come down to deliver them. And now come, I will send you to Egypt." "This Moses whom they rejected, saying, 'Who made you a ruler and a judge?' is the one God sent to be a ruler and a deliverer by the hand of the Angel who appeared to him in the bush. He brought them out, after he had shown wonders and signs in the land of Egypt, and in the Red Sea, and in the wilderness 40 years.

☐ Acts 8:26–27 (NIV)

Now an angel of the Lord said to Philip, "Go south to the road—the desert road—that goes down from Jerusalem to Gaza." So he started out, and on his way he met an Ethiopian eunuch, an important official in charge of all the treasury of Candace, queen of the Ethiopians. This man had gone to Jerusalem to worship....

_____

_____

_____

_____

On the lines above, write revelations received, commitments / vows made, sins revealed and repented of, life directions, callings / gifts / talents discovered, etc.

Your Calling, Election, and Direction
Day 25

Month	*Day*

Prayed ☐   Fasted ☐   Read & Prayed Scripture ☐

☐ Acts 10:3–5 (NIV)

One day at about three in the afternoon he had a vision. He distinctly saw an angel of God, who came to him and said, "Cornelius!" Cornelius stared at him in fear. "What is it, Lord?" he asked. The angel answered, "Your prayers and gifts to the poor have come up as a memorial offering before God. Now send men to Joppa to bring back a man named Simon who is called Peter.

☐ Acts 15:22, 25 (NASB)

Then it seemed good to the apostles and the elders, with the whole church, to choose men from among them to send to Antioch with Paul and Barnabas—Judas called Barsabbas, and Silas, leading men among the brethren....It seemed good to us, having become of one mind, to select men to send to you with our beloved Barnabas and Paul....

☐ Acts 22:21 (AMP)

And the Lord said to me, Go, for I will send you far away unto the Gentiles (nations).

☐ Acts 26:15–17 (NKJV)

So I said, 'Who are You, Lord?' And He said, 'I am Jesus, whom you are persecuting. But *rise* and stand on your feet; for I have appeared to you for this purpose, to make you a minister and a witness both of the things which you have seen and of the things which I will yet reveal to you. I will deliver you from the Jewish people, as well as from the Gentiles, to whom I now send you....

☐ Romans 10:15 (NIV)

And how can they preach unless they are sent? As it is written, "How beautiful are the feet of those who bring good news!"

☐ Romans 11:29 (NASB)

For the gifts and the calling of God are irrevocable.

_____

_____

_____

_____

On the lines above, write revelations received, commitments / vows made, sins revealed and repented of, life directions, callings / gifts / talents discovered, etc.

Your Calling, Election, and Direction
Day 26

_____   _____
Month   ***Day***

Prayed ☐   Fasted ☐   Read & Prayed Scripture ☐

☐ 2 Thessalonians 1:11 (NIV)

With this in mind, we constantly pray for you, that our God may count you worthy of his calling, and that by his power he may fulfill every good purpose of yours and every act prompted by your faith.

☐ 2 Timothy 1:9 (NASB)

Who has saved us and called us with a holy calling, not according to our works, but according to His own purpose and grace which was granted us in Christ Jesus from all eternity....

☐ 1 Peter 2:9–10 (AMP)

But you are a chosen race, a royal priesthood, a dedicated nation, [God's] own purchased, special people, that you may set forth the wonderful deeds and display the virtues and perfections of Him Who called you out of darkness into His marvelous light. Once you were not a people [at all], but now you are God's people; once you were unpitied, but now you are pitied and have received mercy.

☐ 1 Peter 3:8–11 (NKJV)

Finally, all of you be of one mind, having compassion for one another; love as brothers, be tenderhearted, be courteous; not returning evil for evil or reviling for reviling, but on the contrary blessing, knowing that you were called to this, that you may inherit a blessing. For "He who would love life And see good days, Let him refrain his tongue from evil, And his lips from speaking deceit. Let him turn away from evil and do good; Let him seek peace and pursue it.

☐ 2 Peter 1:10 (NIV)

Therefore, my brothers, be all the more eager to make your calling and election sure. For if you do these things, you will never fall....

_____

_____

_____

_____

On the lines above, write revelations received, commitments / vows made, sins revealed and repented of, life directions, callings / gifts / talents discovered, etc.

Temptation & Trials

The Scripture for the next seven days will focus on temptation and trials that will come upon all that dwell on the earth to try them, according to Revelation 3:10. The devil, which is the accuser of the brethren, makes accusations against us before God, that he may tempt us. In Job 1:8–12, Satan came before God to accuse Job of worshipping God because of his blessings and protection over him and all that he had. Of course, God allowed Satan to take what Job had and to touch his body with a disease to prove his accusations were false. Through his circumstances, Job sinned not and continued to worship God. Through this biblical example we learn that our trials could be a test to show Satan that we are serving and worshipping God because we love Him and not because of what He is doing for us. Trials are hard because of the unknown, but this is when we should trust God. If we overcome and prove God's Word and remain faithful as Job did, we will be rewarded; if not, we will suffer loss. If we do not pass a test (or trial), we may have to take it again and again until we do. A passed *test* will produce a *test*imony, but a failed test will only produce misery. Temptation does not come from God but comes from the one that desires only to steal, kill, and destroy. Don't allow yourself to be overcome; be an overcomer.

Temptation & Trials
Day 27

| ***Month*** | ***Day*** |

Prayed ☐   Fasted ☐   Read & Prayed Scripture ☐

☐   Genesis 22:1–12 (NIV)

Some time later God tested Abraham. He said to him, "Abraham!" "Here I am," he replied. Then God said, "Take your son, your only son, Isaac, whom you love, and go to the region of Moriah. Sacrifice him there as a burnt offering on one of the mountains I will tell you about." Early the next morning Abraham got up and saddled his donkey. He took with him two of his servants and his son Isaac. When he had cut enough wood for the burnt offering, he set out for the place God had told him about. On the third day Abraham looked up and saw the place in the distance. He said to his servants, "Stay here with the donkey while I and the boy go over there. We will worship and then we will come back to you." Abraham took the wood for the burnt offering and placed it on his son Isaac, and he himself carried the fire and the knife. As the two of them went on together, Isaac spoke up and said to his father Abraham, "Father?" "Yes, my son?" Abraham replied. "The fire and wood are here,"

Isaac said, "but where is the lamb for the burnt offering?" Abraham answered, "God himself will provide the lamb for the burnt offering, my son." And the two of them went on together. When they reached the place God had told him about, Abraham built an altar there and arranged the wood on it. He bound his son Isaac and laid him on the altar, on top of the wood. Then he reached out his hand and took the knife to slay his son. But the angel of the LORD called out to him from heaven, "Abraham! Abraham!" "Here I am," he replied. "Do not lay a hand on the boy," he said. "Do not do anything to him. Now I know that you fear God, because you have not withheld from me your son, your only son."

☐ Isaiah 7:12 (NASB)

But Ahaz said, "I will not ask, nor will I test the LORD!"

☐ Jeremiah 17:9–10 (AMP)

The heart is deceitful above all things, and it is exceedingly perverse and corrupt and severely, mortally sick! Who can know it [perceive, understand, be acquainted with his own heart and mind]? I the Lord search the mind, I try the heart, even to give to every man according to his ways, according to the fruit of his doings.

_____

_____

_____

On the lines above, write revelations received, commitments / vows made, sins revealed and repented of, life directions, callings / gifts / talents discovered, etc.

Temptation & Trials
Day 28

Month	Day

Prayed ☐   Fasted ☐   Read & Prayed Scripture ☐

☐ Matthew 4:1–7 (NIV)

Then Jesus was led by the Spirit into the desert to be tempted by the devil. After fasting forty days and forty nights, he was hungry. The tempter came to him and said, "If you are the Son of God, tell these stones to become bread." Jesus answered, "It is written: 'Man does not live on bread alone, but on every word that comes from the mouth of God.'" Then the devil took him to the holy city and had him stand on the highest point of the temple. "If you are the Son of God," he said, "throw yourself down. For it is written: "'He will command his angels concerning you, and they will lift you up in their hands, so that you will not strike your foot against a stone.'" Jesus answered him, "It is also written: 'Do not put the Lord your God to the test.'"

☐ Matthew 6:9–20 (NASB)

"Pray, then, in this way: 'Our Father who is in heaven, Hallowed be Your name. 'Your kingdom come Your will be done, On earth as it is in heaven. 'Give us this day our daily bread. 'And forgive us our debts, as we also have forgiven our debtors. 'And do not lead us into temptation, but deliver us from evil. [For Yours is the kingdom and the power and the glory forever. Amen.]' "For if you forgive others for their transgressions, your heavenly Father will also forgive you. "But if you do not forgive others, then your Father will not forgive your transgressions. " Whenever you fast, do not put on a gloomy face as the hypocrites do, for they neglect their appearance so that they will be noticed by men when they are fasting. Truly I say to you, they have their reward in full. "But you, when you fast, anoint your head and wash your face so that your fasting will not be noticed by men, but by your Father who is in secret; and your Father who sees what is done in secret will reward you. "Do not store up for yourselves treasures on earth, where moth and rust destroy, and where thieves break in and steal. "But store up for yourselves treasures in heaven, where neither moth nor rust destroys, and where thieves do not break in or steal....

_____

_____

_____

On the lines above, write revelations received, commitments / vows made, sins revealed and repented of, life directions, callings / gifts / talents discovered, etc.

Temptation & Trials
Day 29

---------------------------   ---------------------------
            Month   ***Day***

Prayed ☐   Fasted ☐   Read & Prayed Scripture ☐

☐   Matthew 26:41 (NIV)

"Watch and pray so that you will not fall into temptation. The spirit is willing, but the body is weak."

☐   Mark 1:11–13 (NASB)

And a voice came out of the heavens: "You are My beloved Son, in You I am well-pleased." Immediately the Spirit impelled Him to go out into the wilderness. And He was in the wilderness forty days being tempted by Satan; and He was with the wild beasts, and the angels were ministering to Him.

☐   Luke 4:1–13 (AMP)

THEN JESUS, full of and controlled by the Holy Spirit, returned from the Jordan and was led in [by] the [Holy] Spirit For (during) forty days in the wilderness (desert), where He was tempted (tried, tested exceedingly) by the devil. And He ate nothing during those days, and when they were completed, He was hungry. Then the devil said to Him, If You are the Son of God, order this stone to turn into a loaf [of bread]. And Jesus replied to him, It is written, Man shall not live and be sustained by (on) bread alone but by every word and expression of God. Then the devil took Him up to a high mountain and showed Him all the kingdoms of the habitable world in a moment of time [in the twinkling of an eye]. And he said to Him, To You I will give all this power and authority and their glory (all their magnificence, excellence, preeminence, dignity, and grace), for it has been turned over to me, and I give it to whomever I will. Therefore if You will do homage to and worship me [just once], it shall all be Yours. And Jesus replied to him, Get behind Me, Satan! It is written, You shall do homage to and worship the Lord your God, and Him only shall you serve. Then he took Him to Jerusalem and set Him on a gable of the temple, and said to Him, If You are the Son of God, cast Yourself down from here; For it is written, He will give His angels charge over you to guard and watch over you closely and carefully; And on their hands they will bear you up, lest you strike your foot against a stone. And Jesus replied to him, [The Scripture] says, You shall not tempt (try, test exceedingly) the Lord your God. And when the devil had ended every [the complete cycle of] temptation, he [temporarily] left Him [that is, stood off from Him] until another more opportune and favorable time.

☐ Luke 8:13 (NKJV)

But the ones on the rock are those who, when they hear, receive the word with joy; and these have no root, who believe for a while and in time of temptation fall away.

_____

_____

_____

_____

On the lines above, write revelations received, commitments / vows made, sins revealed and repented of, life directions, callings / gifts / talents discovered, etc.

Temptation & Trials
Day 30

_____   _____
Month   Day

Prayed ☐   Fasted ☐   Read & Prayed Scripture ☐

☐   Acts 5:9 (NIV)

Peter said to her, "How could you agree to test the Spirit of the Lord? Look! The feet of the men who buried your husband are at the door, and they will carry you out also."

☐   Acts 20:19 (NASB)

Serving the Lord with all humility and with tears and with trials which came upon me through the plots of the Jews....

☐   1 Corinthians 7:5 (AMP)

Do not refuse and deprive and defraud each other [of your due marital rights], except perhaps by mutual consent for a time, so that you may devote yourselves unhindered to prayer. But afterwards resume marital relations, lest Satan tempt you [to sin] through your lack of restraint of sexual desire.

☐   1 Corinthians 10:13 (NKJV)

No temptation has overtaken you except such as

is common to man; but God is faithful, who will not allow you to be tempted beyond what you are able, but with the temptation will also make the way of escape, that you may be able to bear it.

☐ 2 Corinthians 8:1–7 (NIV)

And now, brothers, we want you to know about the grace that God has given the Macedonian churches. Out of the most severe trial, their overflowing joy and their extreme poverty welled up in rich generosity. For I testify that they gave as much as they were able, and even beyond their ability. Entirely on their own, they urgently pleaded with us for the privilege of sharing in this service to the saints. And they did not do as we expected, but they gave themselves first to the Lord and then to us in keeping with God's will. So we urged Titus, since he had earlier made a beginning, to bring also to completion this act of grace on your part. But just as you excel in everything—in faith, in speech, in knowledge, in complete earnestness and in your love for us—see that you also excel in this grace of giving.

_____

_____

_____

_____

On the lines above, write revelations received, commitments / vows made, sins revealed and repented of, life directions, callings / gifts / talents discovered, etc.

Temptation & Trials
Day 31

Month   ***Day***

Prayed ☐   Fasted ☐   Read & Prayed Scripture ☐

☐ Galatians 6:1 (NIV)

Brothers, if someone is caught in a sin, you who are spiritual should restore him gently. But watch yourself, or you also may be tempted.

☐ 1 Thessalonians 3:5 (NASB)

For this reason, when I could endure it no longer, I also sent to find out about your faith, for fear that the tempter might have tempted you, and our labor would be in vain.

☐ 1 Timothy 6:9 (AMP)

But those who crave to be rich fall into temptation and a snare and into many foolish (useless, godless) and hurtful desires that plunge men into ruin and destruction and miserable perishing.

☐ 2 Timothy 4:5–7 (NKJV)

But you be watchful in all things, endure afflictions, do the work of an evangelist, fulfill your ministry. For I am already being poured out as a drink offering, and the time of my departure is at hand. I have fought the good fight, I have finished the race, I have kept the faith.

☐ Hebrews 2:8–10 (NIV)

And put everything under his feet? In putting everything under him, God left nothing that is not subject to him. Yet at present we do not see everything subject to him. But we see Jesus, who was made a little lower than the angels, now crowned with glory and honor because he suffered death, so that by the grace of God he might taste death for everyone. In bringing many sons to glory, it was fitting that God, for whom and through whom everything exists, should make the author of their salvation perfect through suffering.

On the lines above, write revelations received, commitments / vows made, sins revealed and repented of, life directions, callings / gifts / talents discovered, etc.

Temptation & Trials
Day 32

_____	_____
Month	***Day***

Prayed ☐   Fasted ☐   Read & Prayed Scripture ☐

☐ Hebrews 2:18 (NIV)

Because he himself suffered when he was tempted, he is able to help those who are being tempted.

☐ Hebrews 4:15 (NASB)

For we do not have a high priest who cannot sympathize with our weaknesses, but One who has been tempted in all things as we are, yet without sin.

☐ Hebrews 11:36–37 (AMP)

Others had to suffer the trial of mocking and scourging and even chains and imprisonment. They were stoned to death; they were lured with tempting offers [to renounce their faith]; they were sawn asunder; they were slaughtered by the sword; [while they were alive] they had to go about wrapped in the skins of sheep and goats, utterly destitute, oppressed, cruelly treated.

☐ James 1:2 (NKJV)

My brethren, count it all joy when you fall into various trials....

☐ James 1:12–14 (NIV)

Blessed is the man who perseveres under trial, because when he has stood the test, he will receive the crown of life that God has promised to those who love him. When tempted, no one should say, "God is tempting me." For God cannot be tempted by evil, nor does he tempt anyone; but each one is tempted when, by his own evil desire, he is dragged away and enticed.

☐ 1 Peter 1:6–7 (NASB)

In this you greatly rejoice, even though now for a little while, if necessary, you have been distressed by various trials, so that the proof of your faith, being more precious than gold which is perishable, even though tested by fire, may be found to result in praise and glory and honor at the revelation of Jesus Christ....

_____

_____

_____

_____

On the lines above, write revelations received, commitments / vows made, sins revealed and repented of, life directions, callings / gifts / talents discovered, etc.

Temptation & Trials
Day 33

Month	Day

Prayed ☐   Fasted ☐   Read & Prayed Scripture ☐

☐ 1 Peter 4:12–19 (NIV)

Dear friends, do not be surprised at the painful trial you are suffering, as though something strange were happening to you. But rejoice that you participate in the sufferings of Christ, so that you may be overjoyed when his glory is revealed. If you are insulted because of the name of Christ, you are blessed, for the Spirit of glory and of God rests on you. If you suffer, it should not be as a murderer or thief or any other kind of criminal, or even as a meddler. However, if you suffer as a Christian, do not be ashamed, but praise God that you bear that name. For it is time for judgment to begin with the family of God; and if it begins with us, what will the outcome be for those who do not obey the gospel of God? And, "If it is hard for the righteous to be saved, what will become of the ungodly and the sinner?" So then, those who suffer according to God's will should commit themselves to their faithful Creator and continue to do good.

☐ 2 Peter 2:9 (NASB)

Then the Lord knows how to rescue the godly from temptation, and to keep the unrighteous under punishment for the day of judgment....

☐ Revelation 3:10–12 (AMP)

Because you have guarded and kept My word of patient endurance [have held fast the lesson of My patience with the expectant endurance that I give you], I also will keep you [safe] from the hour of trial (testing) which is coming on the whole world to try those who dwell upon the earth. I am coming quickly; hold fast what you have, so that no one may rob you and deprive you of your crown. He who overcomes (is victorious), I will make him a pillar in the sanctuary of My God; he shall never be put out of it or go out of it, and I will write on him the name of My God and the name of the city of My God, the new Jerusalem, which descends from My God out of heaven, and My own new name.

☐ Revelation 3:21 (NKJV)

To him who overcomes I will grant to sit with Me on My throne, as I also overcame and sat down with My Father on His throne.

_____

_____

On the lines above, write revelations received, commitments / vows made, sins revealed and repented of, life directions, callings / gifts / talents discovered, etc.

Power & Authority

The Scripture for the next seven days will focus on the power and authority we have in Christ. Many seek power and authority in the home, in society, and even within themselves. Power is being sought through education, position, wealth, politics, religion, love, fame, abilities, and beauty. All of this is good, but without God, it profits us nothing. These things will only get us to a certain level of power and authority in this life, but none as a *Child of God*. Being a blood-washed Christian gives us power and authority because we can use the name of Jesus, speak the Word of God, and have the Holy Spirit dwelling within us. Whoever we are in this life, what worldly possessions we have obtained or what position we may hold, Christ in us is the true power and authority. The Greek word *ex-oo-see'-ah* translated means the power of authority (influence) and of right (privilege). The English words power and authority, used in the Word of God, are translated from this Greek word. These words are expressed in our freedoms and privileges we have obtained through Jesus. Paul says in 2 Corinthians 3:17 (KJV), "… where the Spirit of the Lord is, there is liberty." Again, he says in Romans 6:22 (KJV), "But now being made free from sin, and become servants to God, ye have your *fruit unto holiness, and the end everlasting life.*" Because we are free from sin and its bondage, we are free to serve God and have been made joint-heirs with Christ. The results are privileges that come from being a Child of God and the ability to influence the world with a godly lifestyle. Even though the world's and the Child of God's view is the same of position and possession, which results in power and authority, they are very much different. The difference is recognizing who we are and what we have in Christ, not just who we are or what we have in society. The ultimate power and authority is to know who you are in Christ with no questions or doubt.

Power & Authority
Day 34

_____   _____
            Month   ***Day***

Prayed ☐   Fasted ☐   Read & Prayed Scripture ☐

☐   Genesis 32:28 (NIV)

Then the man said, "Your name will no longer be Jacob, but Israel, because you have struggled with God and with men and have overcome."

☐   Exodus 18:21–22 (NASB)

"Furthermore, you shall select out of all the people able men who fear God, men of truth, those who hate dishonest gain; and you shall place these over them as leaders of thousands, of hundreds, of fifties and of tens. "Let them judge the people at all times; and let it be that every major dispute they will bring to you, but every minor dispute they themselves will judge So it will be easier for you, and they will bear the burden with you.

☐   Deuteronomy 8:18 (AMP)

But you shall [earnestly] remember the Lord your God, for it is He Who gives you power to get wealth, that He may establish His covenant which He swore to your fathers, as it is this day.

☐ 2 Samuel 22:33 (NKJV)

God is my strength and power, And He makes my way perfect.

☐ 2 Chronicles 25:8 (NIV)

Even if you go and fight courageously in battle, God will overthrow you before the enemy, for God has the power to help or to overthrow."

☐ Psalm 68:35 (NASB)

O God, You are awesome from Your sanctuary. The God of Israel Himself gives strength and power to the people Blessed be God!

☐ Proverbs 18:21 (AMP)

Death and life are in the power of the tongue, and they who indulge in it shall eat the fruit of it [for death or life].

_____

_____

_____

_____

On the lines above, write revelations received, commitments / vows made, sins revealed and repented of, life directions, callings / gifts / talents discovered, etc.

Power & Authority
Day 35

Month	*Day*

Prayed ☐   Fasted ☐   Read & Prayed Scripture ☐

☐ Proverbs 29:2 (NIV)

When the righteous thrive, the people rejoice;
when the wicked rule, the people groan.

☐ Isaiah 40:29 (NASB)

He gives strength to the weary, And to him who
lacks might He increases power.

☐ Daniel 3:26–28 (AMP)

Then Nebuchadnezzar came near to the mouth
of the burning fiery furnace and said, Shadrach,
Meshach, and Abednego, you servants of the
Most High God, come out and come here. Then
Shadrach, Meshach, and Abednego came out
from the midst of the fire. And the satraps, the
deputies, the governors, and the king's counselors
gathered around together and saw these men—
that the fire had no power upon their bodies, nor
was the hair of their head singed; neither were
their garments scorched or changed in color or
condition, nor had even the smell of smoke clung
to them. Then Nebuchadnezzar said, Blessed be

the God of Shadrach, Meshach, and Abednego, Who has sent His angel and delivered His servants who believed in, trusted in, and relied on Him! And they set aside the king's command and yielded their bodies rather than serve or worship any god except their own God.

☐ Daniel 6:22–23 (NKJV)

My God sent His angel and shut the lions' mouths, so that they have not hurt me, because I was found innocent before Him; and also, O king, I have done no wrong before you." Now the king was exceedingly glad for him, and commanded that they should take Daniel up out of the den. So Daniel was taken up out of the den, and no injury whatever was found on him, because he believed in his God.

☐ Micah 3:8 (NIV)

But as for me, I am filled with power, with the Spirit of the LORD, and with justice and might, to declare to Jacob his transgression, to Israel his sin.

_____

_____

_____

_____

On the lines above, write revelations received, commitments / vows made, sins revealed and repented of, life directions, callings / gifts / talents discovered, etc.

Power & Authority
Day 36

Month   *Day*

Prayed ☐   Fasted ☐   Read & Prayed Scripture ☐

☐ Zechariah 4:6 (NIV)

So he said to me, "This is the word of the LORD to Zerubbabel: 'Not by might nor by power, but by my Spirit,' says the LORD Almighty."

☐ Matthew 7:29 (NASB)

For He was teaching them as one having authority, and not as their scribes.

☐ Matthew 9:8 (AMP)

When the crowds saw it, they were struck with fear and awe; and they recognized God and praised and thanked Him, Who had given such power and authority to men.

☐ Matthew 10:1 (NKJV)

And when He had called His twelve disciples to Him, He gave them power over unclean spirits, to cast them out, and to heal all kinds of sickness and all kinds of disease.

☐ Matthew 21:23–24 (NIV)

Jesus entered the temple courts, and, while he was teaching, the chief priests and the elders of the people came to him. "By what authority are you doing these things?" they asked. "And who gave you this authority?" Jesus replied, "I will also ask you one question. If you answer me, I will tell you by what authority I am doing these things."

☐ Matthew 28:18 (NASB)

And Jesus came up and spoke to them, saying, "All authority has been given to Me in heaven and on earth."

☐ Mark 1:27 (AMP)

And they were all so amazed and almost terrified that they kept questioning and demanding one of another, saying, What is this? What new (fresh) teaching! With authority He gives orders even to the unclean spirits and they obey Him!

_____

_____

_____

_____

On the lines above, write revelations received, commitments / vows made, sins revealed and repented of, life directions, callings / gifts / talents discovered, etc.

Power & Authority
Day 37

Month	_Day_

Prayed ☐   Fasted ☐   Read & Prayed Scripture ☐

☐ Mark 6:7 (NIV)

Calling the Twelve to him, he sent them out two by two and gave them authority over evil spirits.

☐ Mark 16:17–18 (NASB)

"These signs will accompany those who have believed: in My name they will cast out demons, they will speak with new tongues; they will pick up serpents, and if they drink any deadly poison, it will not hurt them; they will lay hands on the sick, and they will recover."

☐ Luke 4:14 (AMP)

Then Jesus went back full of and under the power of the [Holy] Spirit into Galilee, and the fame of Him spread through the whole region round about.

☐ Luke 4:32 (NKJV)

And they were astonished at His teaching, for His word was with authority.

☐ Luke 4:36 (NIV)

All the people were amazed and said to each other, "What is this teaching? With authority and power he gives orders to evil spirits and they come out!"

☐ Luke 9:1 (NASB)

And He called the twelve together, and gave them power and authority over all the demons and to heal diseases.

☐ Luke 10:19 (AMP)

Behold! I have given you authority and power to trample upon serpents and scorpions, and [physical and mental strength and ability] over all the power that the enemy [possesses]; and nothing shall in any way harm you.

_____

_____

_____

_____

On the lines above, write revelations received, commitments / vows made, sins revealed and repented of, life directions, callings / gifts / talents discovered, etc.

Power & Authority
Day 38

Month	_Day_

Prayed ☐   Fasted ☐   Read & Prayed Scripture ☐

☐ John 1:12 (NIV)

Yet to all who received him, to those who believed in his name, he gave the right to become children of God....

☐ Acts 1:8 (NASB)

But you will receive power when the Holy Spirit has come upon you; and you shall be My witnesses both in Jerusalem, and in all Judea and Samaria, and even to the remotest part of the earth."

☐ Acts 4:33 (AMP)

And with great strength and ability and power the apostles delivered their testimony to the resurrection of the Lord Jesus, and great grace (loving-kindness and favor and goodwill) rested richly upon them all.

☐ Acts 6:8 (NKJV)

And Stephen, full of faith and power, did great wonders and signs among the people.

☐ Romans 1:16 (NIV)

I am not ashamed of the gospel, because it is the power of God for the salvation of everyone who believes: first for the Jew, then for the Gentile.

☐ Romans 10:12 (NASB)

For there is no distinction between Jew and Greek; for the same Lord is Lord of all, abounding in riches for all who call on Him....

☐ Romans 13:1–2 (AMP)

LET EVERY person be loyally subject to the governing (civil) authorities. For there is no authority except from God [by His permission, His sanction], and those that exist do so by God's appointment. Therefore he who resists and sets himself up against the authorities resists what God has appointed and arranged [in divine order]. And those who resist will bring down judgment upon themselves [receiving the penalty due them].

_____

_____

_____

_____

On the lines above, write revelations received, commitments / vows made, sins revealed and repented of, life directions, callings / gifts / talents discovered, etc.

Power & Authority
Day 39

Month   **Day**

Prayed ☐   Fasted ☐   Read & Prayed Scripture ☐

☐   Romans 13:3–5 (NIV)

For rulers hold no terror for those who do right, but for those who do wrong. Do you want to be free from fear of the one in authority? Then do what is right and he will commend you. For he is God's servant to do you good. But if you do wrong, be afraid, for he does not bear the sword for nothing. He is God's servant, an agent of wrath to bring punishment on the wrongdoer. Therefore, it is necessary to submit to the authorities, not only because of possible punishment but also because of conscience.

☐   1 Corinthians 1:18 (NASB)

For the word of the cross is foolishness to those who are perishing, but to us who are being saved it is the power of God.

☐   1 Corinthians 2:4–5 (AMP)

And my language and my message were not set forth in persuasive (enticing and plausible) words of wisdom, but they were in demonstration of the [Holy] Spirit and power [a proof by the

Spirit and power of God, operating on me and stirring in the minds of my hearers the most holy emotions and thus persuading them], So that your faith might not rest in the wisdom of men (human philosophy), but in the power of God.

☐ 1 Corinthians 4:20 (NKJV)

For the kingdom of God is not in word but in power.

☐ 2 Corinthians 10:8 (NIV)

For even if I boast somewhat freely about the authority the Lord gave us for building you up rather than pulling you down, I will not be ashamed of it.

☐ 2 Corinthians 12:9 (NASB)

And He has said to me, "My grace is sufficient for you, for power is perfected in weakness" Most gladly, therefore, I will rather boast about my weaknesses, so that the power of Christ may dwell in me.

_____

_____

_____

_____

On the lines above, write revelations received, commitments / vows made, sins revealed and repented of, life directions, callings / gifts / talents discovered, etc.

Power & Authority
Day 40

Month   **Day**

Prayed ☐   Fasted ☐   Read & Prayed Scripture ☐

☐ Ephesians 3:20 (NIV)

Now to him who is able to do immeasurably more than all we ask or imagine, according to his power that is at work within us,

☐ Ephesians 6:10–18 (NASB)

Finally, be strong in the Lord and in the strength of His might. Put on the full armor of God, so that you will be able to stand firm against the schemes of the devil. For our struggle is not against flesh and blood, but against the rulers, against the powers, against the world forces of this darkness, against the spiritual forces of wickedness in the heavenly places. Therefore, take up the full armor of God, so that you will be able to resist in the evil day, and having done everything, to stand firm. Stand firm therefore, *having girded your loins with truth,* and *having put on the breastplate of righteousness,* and having shod *your feet with the preparation of the gospel of peace*; in addition to all, taking up the shield of faith with which you will be able to extinguish all the flaming arrows of the evil one. And take *the helmet of salvation*, and the sword of the Spirit, which is the word of God. With all prayer and petition pray at all times in the Spirit, and with this in view, be on the alert with all perseverance and petition for all the saints....

☐ 1 Thessalonians 1:5 (AMP)

For our [preaching of the] glad tidings (the Gospel) came to you not only in word, but also in [its own inherent] power and in the Holy Spirit and with great conviction and absolute certainty [on our part]. You know what kind of men we proved [ourselves] to be among you for your good.

☐ 2 Timothy 1:7 (NKJV)

For God has not given us a spirit of fear, but of power and of love and of a sound mind.

☐ Titus 2:15 (NIV)

These, then, are the things you should teach. Encourage and rebuke with all authority. Do not let anyone despise you.

_____

_____

_____

_____

On the lines above, write revelations received, commitments / vows made, sins revealed and repented of, life directions, callings / gifts / talents discovered, etc.

• • •

Now that your fasting period is over and it is time to eat, consider eating more wisely. The following passages contain foods the scripture allows us to eat, to assist us in maintaining a healthy diet. The listed passages are guidelines only, but in no way intended to set rules for what you should or should not eat. Green plants, fruit trees, plant and fruit seed, grains, land animal meats, honey (some sweets), fresh water and sea water fish with fins and scales, and bread are some of the foods mentioned to eat, but it is not an all-inclusive list. Leviticus 11 lists dietary restrictions for the people of Israel, but in the New Testament, the rules were changed for the Church according to these passages: Acts 10:9–16, Romans 10:4, Romans 14:1–23, Galatians 3:24–26, and Ephesians 2:15.

As a New Testament Child of God, you have the right to eat whatever you want as long as it does not cause another to stumble or is not harmful to your own body. Today, Christians should have two concerns; how much we eat, or are we over-indulging in a particular food that may be harmful to our health. The ability to control ourselves is reflected in our physical appetites. If these appetites are unable to be controlled, then our ability to control our minds and mouths will also be out of control (Deuteronomy 21:20, 2 Corinthians 10:5–6, and 2 Timothy 3:1–9). Fasting is a discipline that will assist us to gain and retain control over the lust of the eye and of the flesh.

In this world of medical advances, technological breakthroughs and a heightened awareness of fitness education, there should be no excuse why we cannot live a healthier lifestyle. With better eating habits and the availability of great healthcare, you can have longevity with quality of life. The purpose of this section is to raise an awareness to eat better and take care of the only body (vessel) you will ever have. Remember, your body is the temple of the Holy Spirit (1 Corinthians 3:16, NIV) "Don't you know that you yourselves are God's temple and that God's Spirit lives in you?" (1 Corinthians 6:19, NIV) "Do you not know that your body is a temple of the Holy Spirit, who is in you, whom you have received from God? You are not your own...."

☐ Genesis 1:29 (NIV)

Then God said, "I give you every seed-bearing plant on the face of the whole earth and every tree that has fruit with seed in it. They will be yours for food."

☐ Genesis 9:3–4 (NASB)

"Every moving thing that is alive shall be food for you; I give all to you, as I gave the green plant. Only you shall not eat flesh with its life, that is, its blood."

☐ Deuteronomy 8:7–9 (AMP)

For the Lord your God is bringing you into a good land, a land of brooks of water, of fountains and springs, flowing forth in valleys and hills; A land of wheat and barley, and vines and fig trees and pomegranates, a land of olive trees and honey; A land in which you shall eat food without shortage and lack nothing in it; a land whose stones are iron and out of whose hills you can dig copper.

☐ Leviticus 3:17 (NKJV)

'*This shall be* a perpetual statute throughout your generations in all your dwellings: you shall eat neither fat nor blood.'"

☐ Leviticus 11:9–12 (NIV)

"'Of all the creatures living in the water of the seas and the streams, you may eat any that have fins and scales. But all creatures in the seas or streams that do not have fins and scales—whether among all the swarming things or among all the other living creatures in the water—you are to detest. And since you are to detest them, you must not eat their meat and you must detest their carcasses. Anything living in the water that does not have fins and scales is to be detestable to you.

☐ Deuteronomy 14:9 (NASB)

These ye may eat of all that are in the waters: whatsoever hath fins and scales may ye eat....

☐ Luke 24:40–43 (AMP)

And when he had said this, he showed them His hands and His feet. And while [since] they still could not believe it for sheer joy and marveled, he said to them, Have you anything here to eat? They gave him a piece of broiled fish, And he took [it] and ate [it] before them.

☐ John 21:13–14 (NKJV)

Jesus then came and took the bread and gave it to them, and likewise the fish. This *is* now the third time Jesus showed himself to His disciples after he was raised from the dead.

_____

_____

_____

_____

On the lines above, write revelations received, commitments / vows made, sins revealed and repented of, life directions, callings / gifts / talents discovered, etc.

• • •

Use the following sheets for additional space to record your writings during your prayer and fasting.

Write your revelations,
directions, commitments, etc.,
in the spaces below   *Day and time*

1. _____ _____

2. _____ _____

3. _____ _____

4. _____ _____

5. _____ _____

6. _____ _____

7. _____ _____

8. _____ _____

9. _____ _____

10. _____ _____

11. _____ _____

12. _____ _____

13. _____ _____

14. _____ _____

15. _____ _____

16. _____ _____

17. _____ _____

18. _____ _____

19. _____ _____

20. _____ _____

21. _____ _____

22. _____ _____

23. _____ _____

24. _____ _____

25. _____ _____

26. _____ _____

27. _____ _____

28. _____ _____

29. _____ _____

30. _____ _____

31. _____ _____

32. _____ _____

33. _____ _____

• • •

Write prayer requests in the spaces below.

1. _____

2. _____

3. _____

4. _____

5. _____

6. _____

7. _____

8. _____

9. _____

10. _____

11. _____

12. _____

13. _____

14. _____

15. _____

16. _____

17. _____

18. _____

19. _____

20. _____

21. _____

22. _____

23. _____

24. _____

25. _____

26. _____

27. _____

28. _____

29. _____

30. _____

31. _____

32. _____

33. _____

Every day of my forty days of prayer and fasting, I prayed for each request I started with.

Yes ☐ No ☐

For each added request, I prayed every day for the remainder of my forty days of prayer and fasting.

Yes ☐ No ☐

• • •

In the space below, write praise reports for answered prayers that correspond to the prayer requests from the previous page.

1. _____

2. _____

3. _____

4. _____

5. _____

6. _____

7. _____

8. _____

9. _____

10. _____

11. _____

12. _____

13. _____

14. _____

15. _____

16. _____

17. _____

18. _____

19. _____

20. _____

21. _____

22. _____

23. _____

24. _____

25. _____

26. _____

27. _____

28. _____

29. _____

30. _____

31. _____

32. _____

33. _____

• • •

Write the names of the people from your church or group who are participating in prayer and fasting with you.

	Other information about the prayer & fasting participant
Name	

1. _____ _____

2. _____ _____

3. _____ _____

4. _____ _____

5. _____ _____

6. _____ _____

7. _____ _____

8. _____ _____

9. _____ _____

10. _____ _____

11. _____ _____

12. _____ _____

13. _____ _____

14. _____ _____

15. _____ _____

16. _____ _____

17. _____ _____

18. _____ _____

19. _____ _____

20. _____ _____

21. _____ _____

22. _____ _____

23. _____ _____

24. _____ _____

25. _____ _____

26. _____ _____

27. _____ _____

28. _____ _____

29. _____ _____

30. _____ _____

31. _____ _____

32. _____ _____

33. _____ _____

Every day of my forty days of prayer and fasting, I prayed for each person in my group.

Yes ☐ No ☐

• • •

Use this page for additional writings.

1. _____

2. _____

3. _____

4. _____

5. _____

6. _____

7. _____

8. _____

9. _____

10. _____

11. _____

12. _____

13. _____

14. _____

15. _____

16. _____

17. _____

18. _____

19. _____

20. _____

21. _____

22. _____

23. _____

24. _____

25. _____

26. _____

27. —————————————————————

28. —————————————————————

29. —————————————————————

30. —————————————————————

31. —————————————————————

32. —————————————————————

33. —————————————————————

34. —————————————————————

35. —————————————————————

36. —————————————————————

37. —————————————————————

Contact:

Daniel W. Evans
Divine Touch / Daniel Evans Ministries
P.O. Box 61075
Durham, NC 27715
www.danielevans.org